# Birthing The Babes of the Light

A co-creation of inspired poems and drawings, messages,

prayers, and introduction brought forth by *Our Ascended Dear Ones:*

**Lady Master Portia, Beloved St. Germaine, Beloved Mother Mary,**

**Lord Sananda, Sanat Kumara, and El Morya.**

## Penelope A. Greenwell

*Published by*

**Pentangle Press**
Pagosa Springs, CO 81147 / (970) 731-9559

ISBN 0-9648147-8-1

First printing, October 1995

Cover and interior illustrations: Penelope A. Greenwell

Book design: Ben Rayfield

Editing: Sara Benjamin Rhodes

Printed in America by Becotte and Gershwin
Warminster, PA

# Table of Contents

# In Gratitude

With all my heart and great love I wish to thank all who have participated in the co-creation of this book — this great effort from many individualized beings on both sides of the veil, some of whom I am aware and others of whom I am not: to all those who have come before me, who have held the focus for evolution and the Divine Plan, preparing the path and leaving the patterns in myth, art, and the written word; to my parents for co-creating my vehicle and helping me to learn the ways of the third dimension; to the Spiritual Hierarchy and all the Beings of Light who assisted these transmissions and held the focus for their birthing into form; to my guides and sponsors for guiding and assisting me in my lessons, for unfathomable patience and persistence; to Joel for recognizing me, even though I did not understand, and beginning my journey of mastership; to Joanie, Elizabet, Bill, Dudley, Chris, Indigo, and Mark for a view of and a chance to play with those who "walked their talk" and allowed Spirit to prevail; to Len and Lori for helping me to "see" myself, meet the masters, and awaken the Spiritual Midwife and co-creator; to Rachel for endless hours and patience, holding the focus, soothing my body and transcribing tapes; to Jayn and Flo for editing, perspective and sisterly love; to Glenda for encouragement, guidance, and impeccable timing and clarity; to all the sisters for holding the focus for the dream; to my children for giving me the experiences and knowledge which created a perception that this possibility could become; to Victoria for understanding the Mother and careful discernment; to Sara for exquisite editing and the guidance of a hawk's eye view; to Ben for his touch from the Center and the artful design and focus that allowed the words and pictures to take form with the dignity and balance deserving of the Masters and the Hierarchy; to the Babes of the Seventh Manu for giving me the opportunity to welcome you home to Mother Earth; and to St. Germaine, Portia, Mary, Sananda, Claire, El Morya, and Sanat Kumara for honoring me with their vibration and messages of wisdom and hope, for sponsoring this material across the void into form. I pledge my love and support to all of you in the continued unfoldment of the vibration of the Seventh Manu — the promise of the New Age of Spiritual Freedom.

# Dedication

To my greatest teachers, my four children:
who have molded me into shape,
who have been demanding and tenacious
and the clearest reflection of truth:

*The Capricorn Poet,*
never afraid to jump off mountains,who sees the wonder in all
and delights in feeding me with delicacies from other realms.

*The Gemini playful warrior,*
who is never afraid to move faster than light,
who taught me how to say no and the importance of boundaries,
unconditional love, and dancing.

*The gentle Aries mirror*
whose innocence and order, mystify and enrapture all
as she creates spaces for co-creation of love, beauty, and respect.

*"God's gift to the world", the sage Scorpio,*
who speaks a language known to few of truth and determination,
who will translate the wisdom of the animals.

*May all parents receive as much love and learning as I do from my children,*
*may all the children of the new generations live in the love, light, and wisdom*
*that bathes them through their struggles and trails,*
*may "we all build a road that will take us where we want to go…"**

---

\* paraphrased from Acoustic Junction's song, Build A Road, Reed Foehl, from *Love It For What It Is*, Planet Records, 1991.

All of this material is inspired and influenced by the Masters of Breath, Sound and Light who sponsored it. As all is channeled and inspired material, it is filtered through the personality and perspective of the mind through whom it is received. To distinguish, the direct channelings are in italics, my writings and explanations are not. Parenthetical statements or asides by the speaker of a passage are in ( ), whereas [ ] denote insertions or clarifications by myself or the editor, Sara Benjamin Rhodes. The poems and drawings are not attributed to a particular vibration, rather considered to stand under my authorship as primary. I have been asked by St. Germaine to copyright the material, to serve as protector of its purity and clarity, I will consider requests of pure intention for reproduction with attribution. The punctuation and phrasing is often unusual in the poems. They are meant to be read aloud, as such you will find they activate new paradigms for the mind and emotions. Try reading the prayers out loud also, the energy parameters are very powerful. The whole time I was receiving the channelings and writing the poems I knew there were to be drawings, However I couldn't see the images. The symbols came easily and finally when the last poem was written, I saw images that seemed familiar.  I had done similar drawings in 1987-88. I found the old portfolio and was stunned that these were the images. These drawings were done in a very spontaneous way — very compelling images that seemed to appear on the blank page. They came from my hand at a time when I was beginning to understand that I was a vehicle for inspiration, that my art was through me, not of me. As such they represent the birthing of my consciousness as co-creator. A few of the images were added, recently to complete the set. As of yet I do not completely understand them, and the imagery and feelings they evoke, although I know they belong to the work, as a whole.

# Introduction

The experience of co-creating this book has been one of great learning, on several levels. In many ways it mirrors the birthing process it presents as possible. Three years ago I met a gifted healer, teacher, and seer who awakened me to Ascended Masters' teachings. Len Toye quickly taught me a few keys to access universal powers and laws, and I discovered that the great masters I had studied and aspired to emulate — Lao Tse, Buddha, Jesus, Plato, St. Francis, Leonardo, Zoraster, and Ptolemy — were indeed connected, and that their continuum represented an integrated body of teaching which blended art, philosophy, science, and history. The puzzle pieces of my prior experiences and learning began to fall into place. I was ripe for this awakening for various reasons, and having recently surrendered to the inevitability of the workings of, and encounters with, Spirit in my life. I had been praying to receive definition and focus as to my life's work and the exact way to walk my talk NOW. Blessed with the teachings and friendship of Len and his wife Lori, (also a channel and author)[1] my life became a whirlwind of weirdness. I soon began to understand the content and images in the artistic work I had generated for the past fifteen years. I channeled a multimedia installation on awakening, self-healing and awareness, *Gabriel's Garden*. I continued the quest for integration, and sought to fit the pieces into the puzzle of the meaning of life and creation. I began to work on a channeled book, a survival guide for those on a spiritual quest — a handbook to life in the "third density." Artwork, study, assisting others in their healing, workshops, and writing more than filled my days. One day I was lamenting my long-running personal battle of how to allow myself to rest when exhausted, and turned to the pen and page to exorcise and expunge my self-judgment. Having done so, I collapsed on the lawn chair to luxuriate in my newfound freedom to relax. A very powerful voice came forward, demanding attention, and I was given the introduction of this book. Initially, I was confused as to why this information was coming to me as I hadn't been involved in birthing for many years. However, I was very grateful to be chosen to receive this information. When I recovered from the shock, I began to recognize the blatantly obvious. I am the mother of four children, all birthed in as natural a way as was possible. As an instructor and counselor of childbirth education and nursing mothers' instructor and counselor, I had witnessed many births in various situations.

---

[1]   Lenard Toye is the founder of the School of the Four Pillars, a school of Mastery and Ascension. Lori Wilkins Toye is a channel and the author of the *I AM America Map*, *The New World Atlas*, *& Freedom Star*.

Presently I teach children art, and children often seem to be drawn to my healing practice and workshops. I have been astounded by many of these little ones, especially in the past few years. They seem to be wise beyond their years, often assisting in healing sessions with their parents. With a little prodding, I discovered that most children under five see auras and play with their guides and angels on a regular basis. When my oldest daughter finally agreed to allow me to do energy work with her and she learned of Ascended Masters' teachings, she admitted that her imaginary friends of years gone by were indeed real, and that she had seen "those spinning things and colors around people, but had made it go away." I had been envisioning a series of children's books, imagining how life for kids would be if they never lost their connection to other dimensions. The Masters had been asking me to include the term, "spiritual midwife" on brochures and business cards. The pieces fell in place and "birthed this book."

# The Channel

I look into the Sun, warm
on my face, my vision
flooded with golden yellow.
My feet planted
on the Earth, her rocks and trees
in my blood and bones, anchored,
One with her spirit …

A fuchsia pebble between my eyes,
hold it there. Then tentacles,
limbs stretching out of my mind,
connecting with and into the light,
into all, the wisdom of history,
the consciousness of now.

Electric blue, waves of purple
royal robes enshroud me.
Loins, yellow warmth reaches
magnitude in orange,
cleaves me in two.

Water pours through me
from above, like a torrent.
Fire and ice, earth and light,
in my body and not of it …
Burning and throbbing, cool
and refreshing, connected
above and below,
within and without.

I have struggled with the terms and concept of attribution. The Masters have requested that their names be used and published with the work. I find co-creatorship the best term to use, as this is a joint process. Clearly some of the book is channeled, some is inspired, and some is from my own experience. All of it has poured forth from my hand through the filter of my personality and perceptions, which in turn have been shaped and honed by experiences in this and other lifetimes. It is colored by my friends and relationships, my family, teachers, and my beliefs. I leave you with these quotations as my best explanation:

*I am the vessel. The draft is God's. And God is the thirsty one.*
Dag Hammarskjold

*God, to me, it seems, is a verb not a noun, proper or improper.*
Buckminster Fuller

*Prayer does not use up artificial energy, doesn't burn up any fossil fuel, doesn't pollute.*
Margaret Mead

*Yet, if the Doctrine of the Heart is too high-winged for thee, if thou needs't help thyself and fearest to offer help to others, then, thou of timid heart, be warned in time: remain content with the Eye Doctrine of the Law. Hope still. For if the Secret Path is unattainable this day, it is within thy reach tomorrow. Learn that no efforts, not the smallest — whether in right or wrong direction — can vanish from the world of causes. E'en wasted smoke remains not traceless. A harsh word uttered in past lives, is not destroyed but ever comes again. The pepper plant will not give birth to roses, nor the sweet jasmine's silver star to thorn or thistle turn.*
H. P. Blavatsky, *The Voice of Silence*

*The tree is known by its fruits; and as all Theosophists have to be judged by their deed and not by what they write or say, so all Theosophical books must be accepted by their merits, and not according to any claim to authority which they may put forward.*
H. P. Blavatsky, *The Key to Theosophy*

Personal experiences of birthing and parenting have taught me the power of faith and trust, with a little sprinkle of "mommy's pixie dust." My children have been my best, toughest and most honest teachers. My last two children were born using the LeBoyer method; firsthand, I saw exquisite, peaceful births and the unforgettable look of my daughter's eyes as she gazed at me with full recognition immediately after her entry into this world, and smiled the most blessed smile I have ever seen to date. Children born in this manner are decidedly different, having a confidence, assurance, and knowingness about the world that is often frightening, especially to a parent.

I strongly recommend that you read *Birth Without Violence*, by Frederick LeBoyer. Many hospitals and birthing centers employ these methods and virtually gone is the once common procedure of hanging an infant by the feet and spanking him/her into consciousness. Many midwives now approach birth in a spiritual manner and work with the entire family in preparation for this sacred event.

Birth is often perceived as a death, or "near death experience." This has not been my experience, actually. It is intense, powerful, very hard work, and at times very frightening. My first child's labor and delivery was moderately long (fifteen hours). I succumbed to a spinal block for a few hours midway, only to hate the loss of control of my body, my legs. I demanded that I get no more anesthetic (it wore off in the last eight hours); I could handle the pain if I had my legs. The feeling of consciously experiencing the birth and the elation of meeting my son more than erased the pain and work. My second child's birth was very different. The pregnancy was horrible from the beginning; I was very sick and lost fifteen pounds. Although labor went relatively smoothly and quickly, as they were wheeling me into the delivery room, the baby suddenly shifted and presented her shoulder. I remember thinking that my back might explode. Some very tricky maneuvers by the nurse-midwife, doctor, and myself ensued and ninety minutes later she came into the world, screaming. The doctor told me that both of us would not have survived if I hadn't been alert and guiding the process. I suffered a broken pelvis; my daughter had a difficult infancy. Using hypnotic regression, I have learned that she was affected *in utero* by my ambivalence about being pregnant while trying to raise a nine-month-old and the frequent absences of her father (he traveled extensively for business). She was ambivalent about coming into being!

As I read Dr. Thomas Verny's *Secret Life of the Unborn Child*, I reflected on my own life and my children's pregnancies. I was thrilled that the power and impact of the influence of pregnancy and birth on the life of each of us is being considered now. We have the opportunity to consciously attune to the perfection of the experience — ourselves, our bodies, and the growing Spirit Body of the child — throughout the entire process. Many midwives and spiritual teachers are encouraging families to enlist the guidance of the unborn child; I heartily encourage this.

My personal journey has brought me to a strong conviction to "walk my talk," and to reveal and share my beliefs and musings as a mother, teacher, artist, and author. I have often wondered how we could gently assist our little ones on their chosen paths, without interfering with their lessons and free will. Again, they are our best teachers: "Listen. Listen to us (we often whisper). Smile more, and please follow your heart." [2]

---

[2]    Advise to his parents from unborn baby Spenser

# 1

# A New Way of Birthing

Many of us have experienced the Light — the feeling of being connected to the Source. I experience it in many ways: during meditation; in the state between sleep and wakefulness; while lying in the sun, or when resting after exercise; while daydreaming, staring into space, or gazing at the sky, a fire, or a flower; or in the afterglow of making love. The joy and peace is so profound, we wish it would never end. Some of us remember this feeling from childhood and how resentful and angry we were when adults interrupted us, when we were told to " stop daydreaming and get to work, do something productive!" Often we were labeled as weird, spacy, aloof, or snobs; and yet now we spend thousands of dollars going to seminars and learning disciplines to regain this connection again! Imagine what we'd be like if we were born into this physical world with our connection to the Source unbroken; if birth was a loving, gentle, healing act; if we were encouraged to see the angels and hear whispered lullabies and gentle sounds that mirrored those from the other side. This book is a gentle journey into this possibility: the birthing of a new generation of beings who remain connected to the Source, who come into this plane with full memory of the other realms and the experiences of other lifetimes and other planes. Some of you reading this are already parents of children who have maintained this connection. Some of you may even have maintained it yourselves. I believe you will resonate with this material and I applaud you. If you feel moved to, share your stories with me, as I wish to follow this publication with a compilation of narratives relating the experiences with the Babes of the Seventh Manu. If you are interested in a newsletter please let me know this, also.

I hope that this material serves you in the spirit it was intended.

I AM always of service to you.

*We are moving into the New Age of Spiritual Freedom, birthing a new Manu, where we will truly learn **from** the children, who will take us into a new dimension. You, as the parents of these beings, are being called to accept **your** birthright, that of the co-sponsors of these beings. This position is one you have agreed to (or you wouldn't be reading this). It will require great courage, as you must provide protection and direction for a new way of parenting, a new concept of family — one based on love and acceptance, on the encouragement of the development of an integrated being from birth. It will require the grace to accept lessons from your children.*

St. Germaine

# Trust That all is Perfect ...

*If you are reading this, trust that all is perfect and in Divine Order. Whether you are a part of a couple, a mom or dad-to-be, a single mom, a grandparent or friend, understand that you have come to this consciousness because it is time. Something has brought you to this little book. It may be obvious or not; it is not important. What is important is that you are here, now, allowing the radiance of these pages to wash over your being. We of the Ancient Sisterhoods have come forth to forge a new way. A new motherhood and fatherhood, perfect and inclusive. You will come from all walks of life, you who sponsor the Beings of the Seventh Realm. You may be students of the Light. You may not have any understanding, at this time, of what you are doing. You do know, however, that my words **feel** right. They are awakening you to some purpose you have always felt in your soul: that we can create a perfect, loving, harmonious world, where all can live in peace. Do not fear your role, your intention, as all will unfold with perfect grace if you simply allow. Allow you heart to open. Feel the Flame of Freedom burning bright inside, freedom of self, freedom of devotion, freedom to love mankind, freedom to do for self and others, freedom to birth a new way of being.*

*If you are a parent or a parent-to-be, know that you have been guided here, now, to complete your understanding of who you are, of who your child is. If you are a grandparent, relative or friend to some child, any child, you read these pages to birth your**self** so that you may gracefully support the transition. For in the New Age of Spiritual Freedom, the society will again support and maintain all of its children, bodily and spiritually. You are part of this shift in consciousness. We all are the mothers and fathers of this new generation.*

Lady Master Portia

If we lived in a perfectly functional world, this book would be unnecessary. We would all know fully and completely how to birth and raise children in perfected harmony. If nothing else, the lessons of the Ascended Masters are always non-judgmental and inclusive. Where you are at this moment is perfect, whether you are on top of the mountain, or picking your way over rocks on the path, or lying at the bottom overwhelmed by the thought of getting up. This is the right place for you now. Just accepting this will create a shift. The fear of judgment from others, of self, the fear of loss, the fear of failure — sometimes the fear of just being here — can color our existence, even immobilize us.

Whether you have purified your body and conceived this child consciously in Love, whispering love and invoking the Name of God at the conception, or you are a single mom or dad; whether you are thrilled with this pregnancy, or adopting a child abandoned by its biological parents; or if you have lived on junk food or are a vegetarian, it matters not.

For if your intention is to birth and raise your child so that he or she may gracefully accept his/her birthright as a Child of God, that is what he or she will become.

All of us are made in the Image and Likeness of the Godhead. All of us can become the Masters, the Gods and Goddesses we truly are, if our intention is pure and we choose to walk in Grace. What exactly does Grace mean? Grateful acceptance?

Ponder this for a while. I have found it to be — at the same time — more difficult and essentially easier than it seems at first. The key concepts for me have been **allowing** and **acceptance**.

Often we cannot see what our life is about, from this vantage point. We certainly cannot know everything that our children's lives are to become. We can, however begin to tune into our inner voice and listen. This tiny being you are beginning a relationship with will also speak to you. Call upon the Higher Self of each child; trust what you hear and act upon it with pure intention and the conviction that all is in Divine Order.

# 2

## The Seventh Manu

# The Seventh Manu

*The Seventh Manu are the Beings of Light who have waited until now to come forth in embodiment, for the radiance was not such to support their birth until 1978.[1] These Beings come forth in embodiment, to take on physical form on the earth plane for the first time, to spread the blessings and radiance of the Seventh Ray: mercy, compassion, transmutation, diplomacy, and freedom. These Beings have waited for a very long time to come forth, some as long as 43 million years. During this time they have worked with the Angelic Realm, the Elemental Kingdoms, the Great Cosmic Beings, and in other realms, to learn the teachings they will bring with them. They had to wait until this time for the proper alignment of the planets cosmically, and for the consciousness presently on the planet to support their service.*

*These Beings will know no duality, only harmony. They come forth in perfect love as the way-showers of the fourth dimension. They will complete this cycle. They will live in their entire Being, a peace and balance mankind has rarely seen for the past 42 million years. Many have come before them to prepare the way, to learn the ways of mankind so that they may protect and support these Beings in their infancy in bodily form. You who have chosen to sponsor and support these Violet Babes must understand the special role you play. These Beings come forth with full memory of the Spiritual Realms. They will maintain this connection with only a little help. They will experience this planet as the garden that it truly is. They will see love and beauty in all. Because their belief systems will not support fear and disillusionment, they will encourage peace and harmony and facilitate conscious interaction, cooperation and interdependent behaviors. As they move among the peoples of the planet, their model will support and sustain planetary peace.*

---

[1]  As is always the case, there are a very small number of beings of the Seventh Manu who were born before 1978, who came to anchor in this radiance and to act as guides and way-showers. These are not to be confused with other "lightworkers or "angelic beings" who are also embodied at this time.

[2]  New Age of Spiritual Freedom: The Hierarchy instituted a new dating system which began on the ingress of Aries 1954.

*You, as their parents and sponsors, must surround them with love and encouragement, for this is the food upon which they thrive. Their behavior will initially seem innocent and yet with time you will recognize the depth of their understandings. People will open to them, unconsciously, and begin their personal transformations. These children of the New Age of Spiritual Freedom[2] will light your life and bring a joy that you have never know before. Listen to their hearts. Sing and dance with them. Talk to them of the angels and play with them in the sunshine. Through them you will know the Wisdom of the Universe, the Song of the Spheres. You have been endowed with a blessing few have chosen to accept. Accept this radiance and go in peace to form the families of tomorrow, in perfect harmony and eternal peace.*

St. Germaine

# The Child of the Seventh Manu

*I AM a Bridge Between Two Worlds —*
*one caught in the snare of fear and doubt,*
*the other a Web of Light, open to*
*the possibility of tomorrow.*
*A whole, bound together by love.*
*I walk a treacherous path*
*and yet I know I AM always connected.*
*My existence is the Light;*
*to it I can always return.*
*I AM also the dark —*
*warm and gentle, the cradle —*
*the womb of all birth.*

*I fear not and focus ahead.*
*I have watched you from afar.*
*We have completed agreements*
*that you will  walk me through the door.*
*Be my bridge unto this world!*
*And teach to me its ways,*
*pitfalls and traps,*
*its beauty and wonder,*
*unique in the Universe.*

*Give to me a body,*
*to shield and enfold my Light,*
*to let me feel the joys and sorrows*
*Of Human form and might.*
*For I will become as you, and yet*
*remain connected tight. I will remember*
*always, the angels and the Light. I will*
*bring you eternal joy, wisdom*
*abundance, and insight. Together,*
*we will move the mountains. And create*
*sweet rivers of honey and oceans*
*of the Blood of Life.*
*The world it will become. It must —*
*A haven for us all, the Dove of Life.*
*Spinning, the Heavens will descend*
*on winged songs of Love.*

# 3

## What is a Manu?

# Sananda explains, "What is a Manu?"

*In the beginning of Creation, as we know it, when this world, Terra/Prana (the Earth), was prepared, God sent forth streams of Light Beings, created in His image, to come forth and inhabit this plane, to assist it in its evolution. As each being is breathed out of the Source, it chooses a path of experience, education, and trust. The design for this planet was that there be seven waves of Beings, corresponding to the Seven Rays of Breath, Sound, and Light which comprise the third dimension. Each ray was to be embodied under the sponsorship of a Manu or protector. Each Manu was to have seven subraces, and so on, to reflect the inner and the outer. A lifestream came into embodiment and re-embodied in each subrace (not necessarily in order) until all of the lessons of the Seven Rays were accomplished, all of the attributes mastered. This was originally to be not more than 14,000 years. When all of the attributes of all Seven Rays were completely assimilated and understood, the being had Mastery of the third-dimensional plane and moved on to other realms, having learned the teachings of the third dimension. And so it was that those assigned to the first three Manus progressed through their experiences on the Earth and ascended into the fourth dimension and beyond. All on Earth was peace and bliss, in Divine Order (the myth of the Garden of Eden). Masters walked on Earth and beings came into form without pain and separation. During the height of the Third Manu [of] Unconditional Love and Devotion, representatives of the Lords of Light from the inner realms came and asked if the Beings on Earth would consider taking on some Beings from another world who had decided not to move forward with that planet into the fourth dimension, as their experience and learning had not advanced far enough. Being under the influence of the Third Ray of Unconditional Love and Devotion and never knowing other, Earthlings agreed. These Beings were assigned to the Fourth Manu. Each Manu overlaps the previous one to assure continuity and constant evolution. However, as these Beings came into form their experiences were different from those of the Earthly Beings and they also suffered from separation from their own world. Many Earthlings and priests began to doubt and question the decision. This is the pivotal point, the introduction of doubt and fear. [A] schism tore at the one-mindedness of the priesthoods, and the Masters and guides had to withdraw from the Earth plane because their consciousness did not include discord. They would continue their sponsorship and guidance, but must do so from afar. For the first time, Earthlings experienced separation from the Godhead. Disputes began to arise as to which priesthood represented the true God and some of* the priesthoods began to exert control of their subjects by requiring allegiance and alms for support and performance of rituals which [supposedly] assisted in reconnection to the Source. Wars, deceit and corruption began to be known on Earth. The Lords of Light saw that man had created this situation out of doubt and lack of trust in the Divine Plan. They saw that man must experience separation from the Godhead and dis-integration of the male and female [aspects of him/herself, both internally and externally] in order to make a **conscious** choice for re-**member**-ship into an integrated reality where all is one, [and where] the individual is an important and sacred functioning part of the whole. Beings who had disobeyed Universal Laws agreed to reincarnate repeatedly, to fully learn the lessons of the Seven Rays. The Karmic Board was devised to assist in the designing of parameters for each embodiment. The Third Manu, because of its memory of a time of bliss and oneness, was able to move through its lessons of the third dimension The Fourth Manu, however, has had a much more difficult time. Forty-two million years later, there are beings now on this Earth who are caught in this cycle of re-embodiment. Long having forgotten their connection to [the Source] and focused entirely on a reality based on illusion, a time/space continuum where they forgot the eternal soul and the interconnectedness of all life in the Universe. Caught in the density of matter precipitated into form, they have repeatedly returned to Earth, ignoring their original plan to learn the lessons of all the Rays. Even the concept of reincarnation was forgotten, beings believing each life had no connection to anything else. Asleep to their immortal true selves, they have not been able to access the wisdom and lessons of the experiences of past lifetimes. The male and female aspects of each being are rarely integrated in the individual being. God, always merciful and forgiving, was considered wrathful and vengeful, reflecting belief systems sustained by self-blame, fear, and doubt. The Fifth and Sixth Manu came into form and few beings have progressed to Mastery of the third dimension. Therefore the Earth is crowded and caught in dis-pair (without the pairing or coming together and balancing of male and female within the individual). Repeatedly, the Lords of Light have sent messengers, prophets, and Masters with teachings designed for the appropriate time. Their teachings are contained in the various religions of all the cultures. But in most cases, forces came forward to control the words and the true meaning of religion (re: to go back to, legion: from legos, the connection)[1] to go back to the connection, to reconnect. I came forward two thousand years ago as Jesus (from the

---

[1] This is Lord Sananda's aside. The origin of this word is not commonly agreed upon.

*Fifth Manu) as the World Teacher for the Sixth Manu. My teachings included reincarnation, mastery, and ascension and encompassed 144 volumes. The priesthoods suppressed or burned all but the one volume you know as the Bible, which contains the teachings encoded in the vernacular of the Roman church. The consciousness of Earth was not prepared for the Truth, but the vibration was established and now, two thousand years hence, the essence of these teachings is becoming acknowledged. The godliness and divinity of each human, if recognized and allowed to manifest, will awaken the soul to its true being. A re-membrance to the family of HUman[2] will allow one to reconnect to the Source, the Mother and Father, to one's past lives and experiences, and to re-collect the path of Godliness and Ascension. The Earth is female in nature and the original plan was that HUman was created to embody the connection between the female (Earth: the Goddess) and the male (God: the Sun, the Celestial Realm). The progression of the Third Manu, Unconditional Love and Devotion (a female vibration) was remembered as the retreat of the Goddess, as these ages of deceit and maljustice ensued. Missing the nurturance of the female and blaming the decision (to take on separated beings) [on her] and [then to] retreat, man rejected the teachings of the female and attempted control of her. As there is no ultimate control over nature, the Earth has progressed in her evolution. Often it is difficult to acknowledge this. At this moment, she is the focus of much attention from the entire Universe. As the radiance of the Seventh Ray (as exemplified in the birth of Beings of the Seventh Manu) comes forward and its attributes — mercy and compassion, freedom, democracy, ritual and celebration — awaken and allow the Earthlings caught here to forgive themselves, God, and his messengers, they [the Earthlings] will release themselves from useless belief systems of fear and doubt and move forward in their evolution.*

---

[2]  Human: Hu is the sanskrit word for God so Human means Godman.

*The birth process reflects the belief systems governing the lifetime of an individual. Whatever one believes of life on Earth — difficulty, pain, violence, peace or joy — this is reflected in the birth. The Babes of the Seventh Manu are freed from karma, and as such have no memory except bliss and peace. Birth for them can be soft, loving, and joyous, if we can put aside our belief in other [illusions created by doubt and fear] and allow the radiance [of these Babes] to swallow our suffering and pain. We as their parents and sponsors, create vehicles of transition for them. How we view their birth will determine the outcome. By allowing peaceful births, we are acknowledging their birthright and re-calling our own. We have the opportunity to transmute the fear and doubts of eons and transit gently into the New Age of Spiritual Freedom.*

Lord Sananda

# 4

## Conception

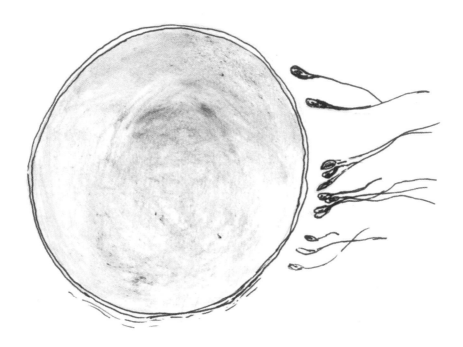

# Twelve Plus One

A pregnancy is a sacred act of allowing.
Allowing a body to grow inside of yours
Protecting it infinitely with the shell of your being.
Allowing your body to change and accommodate
its form.  Breathing its breath, its blood yours.
HUmans come forth from the union of
male and female, a total union,
an immersion in Love. Even
if for just only a moment. One blessed moment.
Thirteen cells — twelve plus one,
divinely prepared, begin to dance.
The selection of one to merge, engulfed by another.
Female enfolding male to become a new
separate being. From two,
shall come one. Unique,
perfect — of the One
Cells divide, multiply,
programmed perfectly, to grow
the form for a Being, perfect —
Unified, One of the Light.

*My Dear Ones I wish to introduce a one, very dear to me: Claire the Elohim of the Fourth Ray. She will speak to you of the amazing plans and designs represented by conception, as you know it in the physical realms. I worked with the Elohim for many years as a child, myself, as they guided me in the understandings of focus and projection that are required for me to hold the pattern of perfection for the Christ. This immaculate concept is required at each birth and for each parent. If addressed consciously, it can greatly smooth the path of parenthood, for all children raised by parents who consciously hold a plan or image of perfection for their child in accord with the Higher Self of the child will treat this child with honor and respect. They will recognize the God within and carefully guide, protect and nurture the potentials for the being, at all times. The Elohim and the Elemental Kingdom hold these immaculate concepts or plans and patterning for each and every thing in form. If you begin to be aware of their presence and acknowledge their contributions, and work with them in conscious union, you will speed your own path and lessons as a co-creator.*

Mother Mary

*My Dear Ones, conception is the advent of life, that moment when the merging of the male and female principles are at their height. If the timing is correct [in a woman's reproductive cycle], it presents an opportunity for a soul to incarnate in physical form. At the moment of highest merging, correctly timed, a specific radiation is emitted which alerts the Celestial Realms that this is an impending opportunity for incarnation. If a soul comes forward whose purpose and goals match the potentials of this possible genetic design parameters, the soul will make contact with the Higher Selves of the mother and father and an agreement will be made. The female must agree to accept this event, this forging of a new life — a new body — to be created by her ovum, the father's seed and the intention of the incarnating soul. When this agreement is reached, the egg is deemed prepared and emits a radiation and the proper chemistry and magnetism which attracts the father's seed to it. Twelve sperm approach the outer rim of the encasement of the egg (the zona pellucida) and, by dancing about it in a specific pattern, electrically activate a portion of the wall. Each sperm, in essence, introduces itself and its potentialities. The incoming soul is in constant communication with both the egg and the sperm and determines the appropriate sperm to represent the DNA blend which most closely meets its incarnation parameters and requirements. When the appropriate seed is found, the signal will be delivered to the ovum which will permit one sperm to enter the wall. It must be understood that all twelve sperm participate in the activation of the zona pellucida. This design is re-presented in many ancient rituals, accords, councils, and decision-making bodies, because it is a basic encoding of life in this dimensional strata.*

# On Conception

*Once the sperm is allowed to penetrate the wall, it is engulfed by the egg and the dance of life begins. The father's seed holds the binary encoding which determines the mitosis or cell division and adds the electronic activation for the polarity to become activated. The ovum lends the encoded sequence which determines how the life stream will be represented in physical form. Both are required, neither can function alone (except in remote cases of immaculate conception or cloning). If there is not adequate determined focus on the part of both parents, the developing child will be affected. One must remember that the incoming lifeform (soul) determines the genetic make up; the size, sex, and characteristics of the physical body into which it will be born. It, in essence, co-creates this form with the Mother and Father. Once conception has been achieved, the light force of the soul and the Mother[female principle] oversee the growth and determination of the physical body. If this is a conscious act — the actual mother and father awakened to their male and female essence and participating fully — the light force will seem very present and the parents may begin a relationship with the being before birth. The soul or Light Being of the incoming life does not fully enter the body of the child until the point of crowning during the transition (the crowning of the being as an incarnate life stream), during the birth process. There are times when the soul will seem very present and at a time between four and six months will energetically cord with the growing body for animation. If a pregnancy is terminated for spontaneous or other reasons, this soul may be approached and contacted for consultation and agreement. The children of the Seventh Manu, at this time, must find sponsors and guides who will fully welcome their being. If ambivalence is present on the part of either or both parents, these beings will often decide to postpone the entry into form. The male and female principles as seen by most of you as Father — God, Sun or Celestial Realms — and Mother — Earth ,Mater and Elemental Realms — will always fully participate in this process. It is a marvelous thing when an incarnate set of beings consciously recognizes their individual essences and are therefore able to participate in the sacred incubation period in physical form. We of the Elemental Kingdoms embrace you fully and exhalt your acknowledgment of co-creatorship. We welcome you into the Kingdoms of Heaven on Earth and look forward to continued relationship with you.*

Claire, Elohim of the Fourth Ray

## Conception

*This is a Being of Light, growing*
*inside my perfect body, conceived*
*in desire, growing*
*in Love.*
*A perfect Being, forever,*
*eternally connected to the Light.*
*One of the Mother, the Earth.*
*One of the Father, the Sun.*
*Come forth in perfected embodiment*
*in service to the Light.*

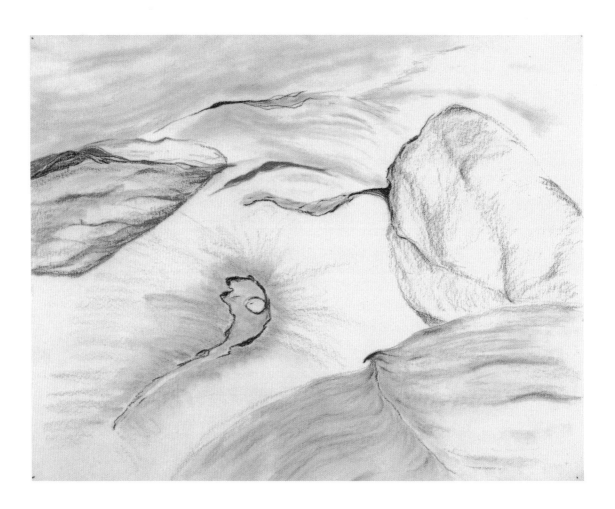

# The Child Speaks

*Dear Mother and Father,*
*Hold the plan of perfection for me,*
*That I might become*
*the Perfected Being that I AM.*
*Shelter me and enshroud me in Love.*
*Blind unconditional Love —*
*the Love of the Mother,*
*the Love of the Father.*

*Do comfort me, correct me.*
*Keep me tight to my path,*
*My purpose in being.*
*Show me the Light and Love in all you do.*
*Surround me in song, comfort, and beauty.*
*Ease my transition into this world,*
*Where we will walk together*
*In service to the One.*
*Listen to me always,*

*Trust what you hear.*
*Echo the Song of Life for me*
*In your actions and deeds.*
*Live your bliss and show me the way.*
*As I AM your Heart's Desire,*
*A reflection of your love.*
*The perfected embodiment of the*
*Divine Will of God.*

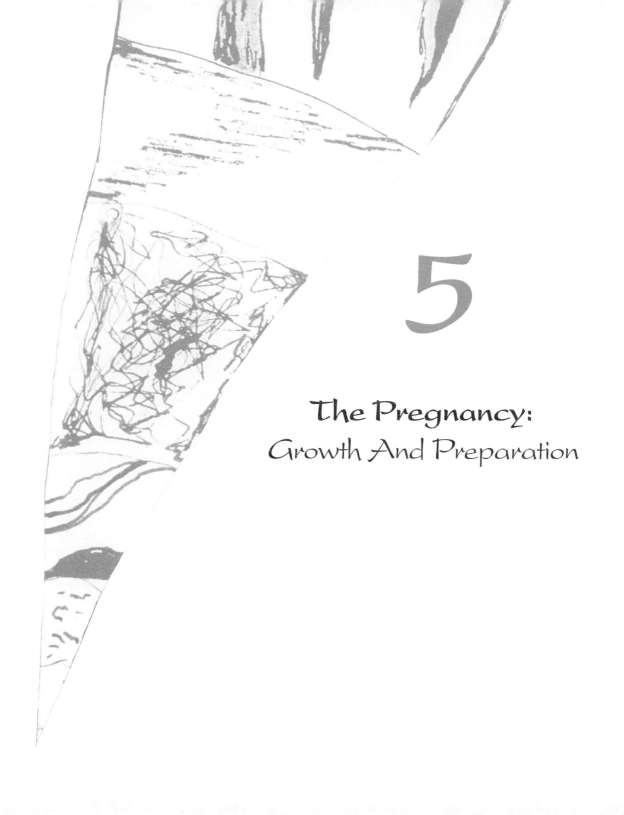

# 5

## The Pregnancy:
Growth And Preparation

# The Sacred Act of Allowing

*Pregnancy, the sacred act of allowing,*
*where one allows your own body*
*to shift and change, to accommodate*
*the creation, growth, and nurturance*
*of another being.*
*In a sense, it is the ultimate perfection of*
*loving service to another.*
*What greater act than to allow*
*your body to accommodate another,*
*to breathe and eat and function as mother!*

*All of your systems centered and tight*
*and focused on nurturing God's holy*
*might. Sustaining, maintaining the Light*
*of this tiny seed becoming, emerging,*
*a mystery indeed.*
*Chemistry changes, new patterns emerge.*
*My body's exploding,*
*it's now really two! Respect*
*you must find for yourself,*
*my love. Honor and nurture*
*this change to the Dove. A sacrifice*
*of self, the merge for another.*

*How can I continue to be? The process
evolving, ever unfolding, mother emerging,
baby becoming … a gift of love
so hard to see.*

*Honor yourself, the Mother, the vessel.
Bless, caress and celebrate a new self
acting in love, embracing creation. Give in
to the magic enfolding your body.
Vibrations of love, bliss, and perfection,
focus and power come forward, as you
give in to sensations that wash
over your body. Heralding the view
of yourself as mother. Droplets of dew
sparkle with blessings, element's form.*

*All that comes is perfect. The sickness,
the nausea, the exhaustion, the discomfort.
Relax and allow, trust of the gnowing,
the growing, the mystery inside. The body
responds with unconscious direction.
I relax into the deep, unknowing trust
of life. All is perfect. The angels
cradle me, soothing
my fears. Surround me,
support me, kissing my ears, release
me to love, trust and devotion, melting
pain and emotion. All is
perfect. I AM the living
embodiment of Love-
in-Action. The perfect action
of allowing, co-creating a new
being for this planet.
One with the Mother, for the Good of Mankind;
One with the Father, Supremely Divine.*

## Instructions to the Father

*Your presence and intention are of grave importance to the success of this endeavor. You as the male hold the focus for the Will of God, the focus and parameters for creation. It was your seed that awoke this egg to become the perfect body for this, your new child. It is you who must protect and hold the focus for perfection conjointly with his/her mother. It is of second nature to you, embodied as a male, to hold the focus for the Light for this being, as it comes into form. Imagine a perfect ray of violet light, streaming down from the sun into the top of your head and flowing into your heart, to blend there with your individual energies and those of the Earth, as you ground yourself to her[1]. Now imagine this Violet Ray streaming forth from your hands, as you stand near the head of your beloved, the mother of your soon-to-be born child. Place your right hand upon her swollen belly; project this light from the center of the palm of your hand, surrounding the entire womb in the most beautiful crystalline violet light. This will accomplish two things. It will attract the Being to the physical body and ease the transition into form, and it will transmute any negative energies immediately, greatly easing your beloved's pain. Imagine you are melting her pain away. You may feel the belly move or spin or contract or soften. Stay with this and, using your intuition, gently move with the body. Imagine the cervix, the vesica pisces, opening wide — the portal from which the infant will emerge down the birth canal. Your left hand can be either on your beloved's heart, at the back of her head, or holding her shoulder or hand. Let her choose, as this is your connection to her. Imagine this violet light streaming forth from this left hand into her being, transmuting all her discomfort into perfect energy to help her push this infant into the world. Breathe with her, filling her with the perfect energy flowing from the Sun and the Earth, through you into her. Tell her of your love for **her** and the joy of this moment. Many women become fiery during the birth process. This is natural. If you both have prepared for this moment — have learned trust and understanding and non-judgment and the movement of energy — all will be accomplished with ease and in due course. Remember at the moment of transition, all movement is heightened, all thoughts, all feelings, all actions are at their most intense. Regulate your breathing and concentrate on your heart. Call forth your guides and the Angelic Realm. Call upon me, for I stand with you and every father at each and every birth.*

---

[1]  See grounding meditation in Appendix B, page 120.

*For each and every Being of this Seventh Manu is sacred and wondrous to me; each one has a special place in my heart, for each must make a separate and individual contribution to the whole. I stand with you, for you as a father, and sponsor of this violet babe, are of vital importance to this New Age of Spiritual Freedom. We, the fathers of a new generation, must forge a new way, the way of the gentle warrior, the patient master and grateful brother, standing shoulder to shoulder with our sisters, as the parents of a new way of being for this world.*

I AM your brother, St. Germaine

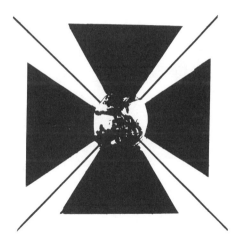

## Dad's Pledge

*I pledge to honor and protect you*
*flesh of my seed.*
*Conceived in Love,*
*without me you would*
*not exist in this form*
*and yet you grow*
*outside me, part of your Mother,*
*my Beloved. You, tiny and vulnerable,*
*challenge my very being.*
*my relationship to her, my purpose.*
*And yet your existence*
*is miraculous.*

*I see my role as protector, to focus*
*on the perfection of your existence.*
*to wonder at the magic,*
*to teach and to guide,*
*to surround you in love*
*and comfort, so that you*
*may grow from a place*
*of strength, of knowing who*
*you are and your place*
*in the Plan.*

*I promise to listen always, respect*
*your being, your essence, no greater*
*or less than my own. We will walk*
*together on this plane, Warriors*
*of Peace, brothers and sisters*
*of the Light, transforming*
*the Planet, in Love and Devotion,*
*from this moment forward.*

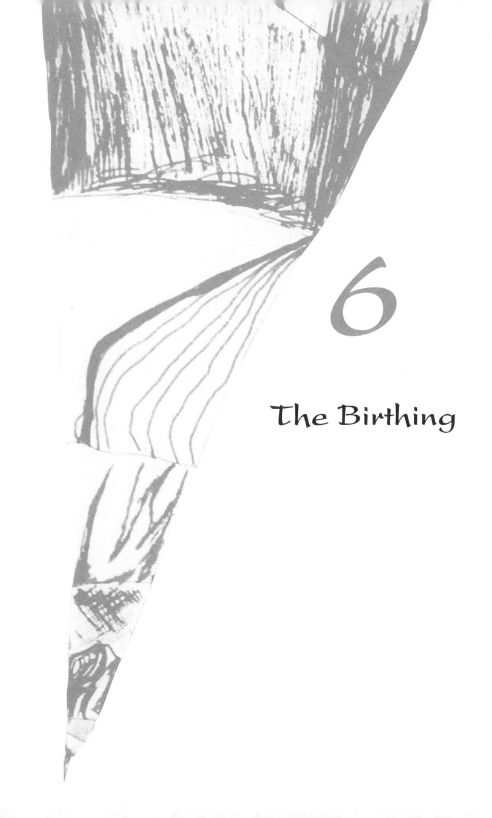

6

## The Birthing

# Do not fear my birth

*Do not fear my birth:*
*Create a space for me.*
*Trust that all will be*
*perfect. Celebrate!*
*Celebrate my coming,*
*Each twinge you feel,*
*quickening*
*in my excitement,*
*awakening*
*my body to*
*Its purpose.*
*Stretching*
*my limbs.*
*Awakening*
*your body.*
*Together*
*we will birth*
*me into form.*
*Leave behind your fear*
*doubt not, speaking*
*of the labor of*
*yesterday.*
*Rejoice!*

Rejoice, today,
for all is new.
Together
we will
create
a new birth
of joyous surrender,
a NEW BIRTH
of Balanced Grace.

Breathe.
Breathe  through.
Breathe your
contractions…Opening
Opening my tunnel
to your arms
The pains,
Intense and sharp
they speak of my
intention.
They speak of
my impatience
to enter your world.

Breathe for me.
Breathe from the
depth of your soul.
Breathe and open
my passage.
Breathe and, expand the Way.
Experience the joy. Allow,
allow me to be.
Trust that our
connection will
always be, always
remain unbroken,
always intact.
I of your body,
you of my soul.
Rejoice in my coming,
fear not the past.
Ease my transition,
Breathe.
Breathe deep of your
knowing.

# The Birthing

*Without the focus of others to assist from the Earth plane at the moment of transition, the Being can become confused, and look to the mother (who is at the height of her vibration, and as light as she has ever been) and forget the connection to the Godhead. This is the cause of duality and separation, even as a metaphor in birth. The babe must be able to look to the Godhead (the Father, light), and look to the Earth (the Mother, Darkness, the birth canal), accept both and remain connected eternally. When this is facilitated by an allowing, a creation of space through focus and determination, when there is no separation, the Being remains of the One, with no separation from unity and therefore has access to the knowledge of ages, all embodiments and the Mysteries of the Ancients. If this connection, this sense of unity — of being One with the Mother (Earth), [and] One with the Father (Celestial Realm, Sun) — is maintained by the parents, the child will never experience separation. The child will be joyful, contented, and fulfilled, feeling whole and assured of his/her place in the grand scheme.*

Mother Mary

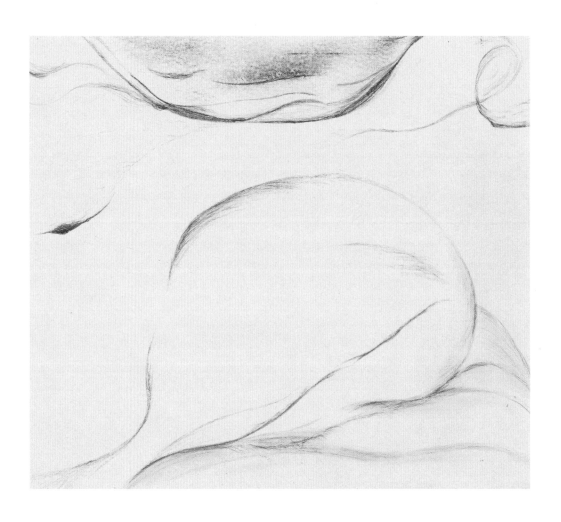

# Love of My Life

*Tiny being growing inside*
*One with the Light, supremely Divine.*
*Grow in perfection, abundance and love,*
*molding my vessel, awakening Dove.*
*Dance in my Being, I enfold you in Light.*
*Breath of my body,*
*flesh of my heart,*
*Come forth in perfection, abundance and love.*
*Wondrous Being, determined and bright,*
*I'll protect you and feed you, Baby of Love,*
*flesh of my Being,*
*Love of my Life.*

# Transition

*I come forward this evening in conjunction with my brother St. Germaine, and our dearest Mother Mary, as we wish to bring to you this information to complete this book on the Seventh Manu. We come forward, Dear Ones, to complete this information and to connect the vibration of Love wholly into this work, to give you the meditations and blessings that will allow these Beings to remain connected, as they come forward in physical form on this plane, at this time. I ask, Dear One, that you bring this information forward in due course, as it is of the highest importance.*

Lord Sananda

The three Beings (Lord Sananda, St. Germaine, and Mother Mary) joined together into a circle, which became a ball of light, often referred to as the Triune of the Holy Family, for Lord Sananda was known in his last embodiment as Jesus, and at the same time, St. Germaine was St. Joseph.  A voice now spoke for the Triune:

*At the point of transition in the birth process on the physical plane  it would be advantageous for a third being to be present at a birth. This will complete the triad of support (with the mother and the father) for the infant, throughout the birth process. This being, as we have called [him/her], is to be the spiritual midwife, to hold the focus for a Being as it comes forward and lowers its vibration into physical form. This point of transition is that point, when the physical form is birthed through the birth canal, that point of transition or movement from the sanctity and safety of the interior of the vessel into the outside world, that point when the Light Being transits the portal.  From the Spiritual Realm this happens as a conjunction, the subtle energetic Light Body comes forward through the portal created by this space called the vesica pisces. The vibration level is lowered into that of the physical form and the Light Being moves forward from the fourth dimension into the third, at the same exact pace and speed as the physical being coming forward through the birth canal. As this being comes forward in  physical form, the Light Being, as we would call it, enters  the physical body. There are two bodies coming through two individual vesica pisces:  one in the physical, third dimension: the body, the head crowned by the cervix, the portal; the other visible through inner or auric vision, coming from the Spiritual Realm, the fourth dimension, also through a vesica pisces or an energetic channel. The Spirit Being enters the physical being through this crowned head, through the "crowned chakra," and merges with it; they are now ONE.  At the point when the baby comes out of the birth canal, they are completely and perfectly joined together, a HUman baby[1]. In the past, as the Being of Light came forward, into this shell of physical form, in most cases, s/he was not able to maintain the connection to the Spiritual Realms except through the Higher Self, or as you would call [it], the Mighty I AM Presence. This spiritual midwife, the mother and/or the father must be able to maintain a focus and intention that the being remain connected, a mental or intuitive, as you would call it, [a] conversation of assurance to the Light Being,*

---

[1] In most all cases — there are a few descrete variations when the light body doesn't completely merge at this point, for a variety of reasons.

*that s/he will maintain the focus as this transition is made. If you can, imagine the importance of projecting and surrounding the energy bodies with radiant energy, as s/he moves forward into this portal. Envision this Light Being is coming forward, the mother and the father and the spiritual midwife triangulating energy to surround the babe for an easy and gentle transition, through the portal, and into the physical body. This will allow the connection to be maintained. We ask Dear Ones, that all project the most pure intention and surround this babe with pink and violet light — the pink representing the vibration of Unconditional Love and Devotion, and the violet representing the Manu or the physical embodiment of this being.[2] The vibration of this being will match the vibration of the Violet Ray. This projection of violet light will act as a homing device or a magnet, greatly easing this transition point. The spiritual midwife, father, or mother may intuit another color which would be that of the personality ray of the being[2]. This intuition is a matter of relaxing and loosing that which you understand to be the limiting forces of the third dimension. As you enter the inner realm of spiritual knowing; you will experience an inner knowing, it may be words, smells, sounds, forms or feelings. Tune into that which you receive, for it will expand and deepen and you will begin to make a connection to the actual Higher Self or guide of the child.*

## The Triune of the Holy Family

---

[2]  Each person also incarnates on a ray which exemplifies the embodiment's work or service.

The Triune now separated out into the three individual beings, and Lord Sananda came forward and spoke: *Dear One, if you use these instructions, this transition will come forward with the greatest of ease and grace and this being will come forth with no pain, as it will remain constantly and inexplicably connected to the source from which it came, the Mighty Godhead. It will remember all its embodiments it will remember its divine purpose, and the great mysteries of life and the creation of mankind. This Being will come forward in absolute and perfect harmony. It will have been attracted in the most perfect way and form. You may add to these words or instructions that which you would intuit at this given point in time. There may be a name that comes forward, there may be further blessings. Each individual birth and each individual moment is a sacred, blessed, unique event, and should be treated as such. It is important that the choice of the individual be considered at all times and the intention be that of true Love and Devotion. These beings come forward on the Violet Ray and vibrate to the frequency of Freedom; they must have the freedom to be born in ways that they individually determine. And now, Dear One I shall step back, as my beloved mother wishes to speak.*

Lord Sananda

# The Prayer of the Cosmos

*I AM Mary and I come forth on that blessed and gentle ray, the Pink Ray of Devotion and Unconditional Love and I speak to you, mother to mother, and I ask that as you proceed with these teachings, that you entwine the color of this exquisite ray in this great work, that you infuse the work with this color (pink) and the symbol of the double rose, representing the unfolding Flower of Life.*

*Dear One, these Beings that come forward now  are of great importance to this New Age and the transition occurring on this Earth. For these Beings, as you understand, come forward to lead the Legions of Light, who will walk shoulder to shoulder, man and woman together, moving forward to fuse the vibrations, to bring forward the infusion of darkness and light, as you have called them, the male and female interwoven together at last, to come forward in freedom, allowing the Violet Star to shine in its exquisite brightness, radiating the qualities of the Violet Ray throughout the Universe.*

*As each being comes into form, and allows its Light Being to be slowed down and [to] enter the physical body which has been so perfectly created for it, as it begins to take his/her breath, embodied as a male or female on this planet, this third party, this silent watcher [the spiritual midwife] comes forward to touch the head and anoint for the first time with a drop of violet essence. This essence may be from any flower which radiates with the violet spectrum: violet, lavender, or lilac [I was shown that the oil is to be put on the baby's forehead at the place of the third eye]. For seven days, this child of the Seventh Manu should be washed with water infused with this essence. After this period of seven days, the oil may be used at the discretion of the mother or father, and it will be found that the child will calm and become happy when washed or anointed [with it]. Instruct the mother and father in this procedure and to bring this babe into the natural sunlight as often as possible.*

*As soon as possible after the birth, speak to this child with these words. This prayer should be repeated at least at each significant event in the child's life, if at all possible every day. Words that invoke the name of God and the name of the child, words always spoken with Love:*

# The Prayer of the Cosmos

I AM the Light of GOD that Never Fails.
I AM an Eternal and Holy Being dedicated to the service of man,
embodied on this Earth in perfected form.
I AM the Song of the Spheres,
I AM the Heartbeat of the Universe,
I AM the Breath of Life,
I AM the Word of God.
I AM……… (name).
I AM the Essence of All,
the Beginning and End, the Alpha and Omega,
I AM pure, perfected, and complete Love.
I AM One with All,
with Mankind,
with the World and all of its Kingdoms.
I AM One with Life.

This, Dear One, is the Prayer of the Cosmos and will awaken all who speak it to their true consciousness, to the true purpose of their Being. Yes, this may also be used for those who have already embodied on the planet in, as you would call it, a rebirthing process into their true purpose. The oil used can be that of the flower of that ray or Manu to which they have embodied. All beings may use the essences of the Violet Ray or the Pink Ray; the essence of rose vibrates with all of life. The Sixth Manu vibrates to the essence of the ruby flowers. The Fifth Manu vibrates to the essences of the grasses, like sweet grass, or sage. The Fourth Manu vibrates to the essence of the white flowers: gardenia, lily of the valley, jasmine. Dear One, these essences should be anointed on these beings in the shape of a cross and a spiral, an eight pointed star and another spiral.

*Dear One, understand that this meditation and that which I gave you previously [see page ] will complete the cycle for this being. If these meditations are performed on a regular basis, to establish a rhythmic and ordered quality in this child's life, s/he will maintain the connection to the Source and ever remember his/her divine purpose. S/he will learn to circulate the energy of this planet through his/her being, connecting always with the energy of the Celestial Realm. S/he will learn to live in that space that we call "Free energy."*[3] *These children must be also taught to regenerate themselves in this way so that they may operate outside of the family unit, using what has been learned in this tiny collective to move confidently throughout the world, in ever-expanding circles and collectives.*

*We wish to thank you, Dear One, for your attention and concentration in this matter. I cannot stress the importance of this information, and I ask — as a personal favor to me, representing the Mothers of the Universe — that you spread this information as rapidly as possible,[by] the means that are available to you. For the more Beings that are brought forward into embodiment who can maintain this connection, the faster the critical proportions will be reached. There have been many who have come forward with interpretations of our teachings and of the prophecies that we have brought forward. There are few who have come forward with the true intention. As you understand, it is our intention to assist in the creation of a world of peace and hope. It is only through clarity, the vibration of clarity that you hold the focus for, that this intention will be kept. [They are showing me a vector, a tube that's clarity.]*

Mother Mary

---

[3]  Free Energy is the space that one attains when one is breathing Prana or Universal Life-force through the base chakra and the crown chakra, connected to male (Sun) and female (Earth) energies. One can sustain life in this space, unconditionally giving forth energy in unlimited supply.  See grounding meditation, Appendix B, page 120.

# Instructions for the Mother

I.   *Center yourself on the place below your heart* (the solar plexus). *Feel the Light within yourself.*

II.  *Breathe regularly and know within you that this birth is new, different from any that have come before.*

III. *Feel the Light in the womb, the perfect vessel you have created for this perfect being. Breathe as you feel it contract, for it is tightening the muscles only to open the portal.*

IV.  *If you breathe deeply with assurance, this will happen more easily. As each contraction eases, feel the baby's body spiraling down the canal.*

V.   *Move your body in any way you feel appropriate. If you wish to stand or walk, do so. Sit or lie down; be on your side or arch your back. Trust that your body will guide you in the movement that is easiest to facilitate the movement down the birth canal.*

VI.  *Allow those assisting you to massage you and radiate energy for you. Bathe and immerse in water as often as possible.*

VII. *Feel the soul of your child; feel the two lights merge into one: your being and that of your soon-to-be-born child. Hold this focus and feel this. Hold this focus and feel this new Being come forward into embodiment, ever connected to the Source, ever connected to you and the Earth.*

Mother Mary

# To Mother,

*Dear One, I have come forward from the Sisterhoods to speak to you further of this birthing process. Ask all involved that you be allowed to guide the process as much as possible. If you are connected to the Source, grounded to the Mother [the Earth] and connected with the soul, the presence of the child, you will act from your intuition and your own bodily needs. It must be explained in preparation, that the breath is what will allow you to remain calm, connected, and virtually without pain. Open the mouth, dropping the lower jaw, which is connected energetically to the pelvic floor [by dropping the jaw you will relax the pelvic floor]. Relax the shoulders. It is important that you have prepared yourself, mentally, physically, and emotionally, if you wish to have a pain-free delivery process; it is always your choice. Breathing, stretching, and strengthening: use movements that are natural to you. Eat foods that are as natural as possible and avoid toxic environments. Try to keep this process as natural as possible, unimpeded by drugs, toxic substances, analgesics or anesthetics, or physical intervention. Rather, prepare and learn the use of breathing and requalifying exercises[4] to erase any negative cause/effect, and/[or] memory of your own birth experience and its impact on this one (this is recommended for the father also). Learn to be proficient in exchanging energy and cycling it with the father or spiritual midwife, to assist in centering and energizing yourself during the difficult points in the labor or delivery.*

*The spiritual midwife needs to be extremely clear; the rebirthing experience is recommended for all, but especially the spiritual midwife. All of this is recommended so that one may allow that to unfold which will serve the highest and most divine purpose for each individual present. Again, I emphasize the importance of allowing the natural process to play out without judgment. Assistance of a midwife schooled in the ancient arts and techniques is most preferable; however, the belief systems of the mother and the father should be respected and honored. Assistance by a being trained in gentle natural birthing procedures may be employed. Ask that being to read this material that s/he may accept this process harmoniously. With preparation and intention, most (if not all) traumatic birth events can be prevented. If, however, one occurs where the infant's body presents itself in reversed or angular position, follow the mother's intuition*

---

4    Requalifying exercises: see Appendix C, page 122.

*in changing her position. Usually if the mother's intuition is allowed to dictate her position early in labor, most mothers will adopt positions to assist the baby's body in its movement smoothly down the birth canal. Her intuition must be tuned and clear: no drugs, substances, or expectations. Use toning and essences and aromas to ease the process. Sounds immediately release emotional and mental patterns. Allow yourself to make whatever tones feel appropriate and good. Trust that whatever occurs is serving a purpose, at times unseen. Call forth support of the Sisterhoods and the Hierarchy. If all individuals remain centered, clearly functioning, and connected, all will be handled in the most appropriate and perfect manner.*

Lady Master Portia

# A Message to Mothers from the Sisterhoods

*Dear One, you are performing the ultimate service to mankind by allowing your body to be the vessel through which a lifestream can embody on this Earth. Honor yourself for this service, and believe that you are worthy of support and assistance. Recognize the knowing within you. Allow your body to guide you, for it has been prepared. Remain focused and connected to the Earth and the center of your being and that of your child. Then look to your beloved: allow him to engulf you with loving support: connect to his heart. Allow a communication with the spiritual midwife. You three will together form the Triune, the magical symbol of creation and manifestation. If another is present for assistance, allow this support to flow also. Speak of your desires clearly, for you are the helmsman, for you maintain the most intimate connection to the infant. Respect your body and its wishes and those of your child. Speak your mind, however trivial it may seem, for any intuition not heeded will come forward eventually for attention. Timely recognition and attention will honor the natural process and allow perfection to come forward. Call forth the power of the Universe at your command. Call forth the Angels and Ancient Sisterhoods, for when you do, you bring forward all the knowledge gained through all the births of all the Beings from the inception of this planet. Call upon your memory and experience in other lifetimes and other realms. Settle yourself in your all-powerful, all-knowing feminine, for this is her greatest hour. This is what the female body is designed to accomplish. Come forth in Love. For the loving essence of the universe will flood your being, soften and ease your resistance and pain, and fuel your strength. Know that I myself, Mother Mary, Kuan Yin, and each and every feminine aspect of the Hierarchy are with you at this time. If you allow it, the power of the Universe is at your command. I give you my special blessing, the blessing of the Ancient Sisterhoods of Opportunity:*

*You, Dear One, come forth in Infinite Perfection*
*Prepared and Awake to the Promise of Tomorrow,*
*Manifesting here in the Now.*
*You are One of the Mother,*
*The Light of the World*
*Born from the Darkness,*
*Sister of the Moon.*
*You stand here today in watchful readiness,*
*Open and Loving,*
*For the Song of the Spheres,*
*Moving through your body, the perfected vessel.*
*Sing with your Heart, completely attuned to the Source.*
*Open yourself, Dear One,*
*to the Song of your Child,*
*a gift of the Universe:*
*Love of my Life,*
*Light of my Heart*
*Babe of the Night*
*Child of the Day*
*Come Forward Now*
*And Light up my Life,*
*Oh, Babe of the Violet Ray.*

Lady Master Portia

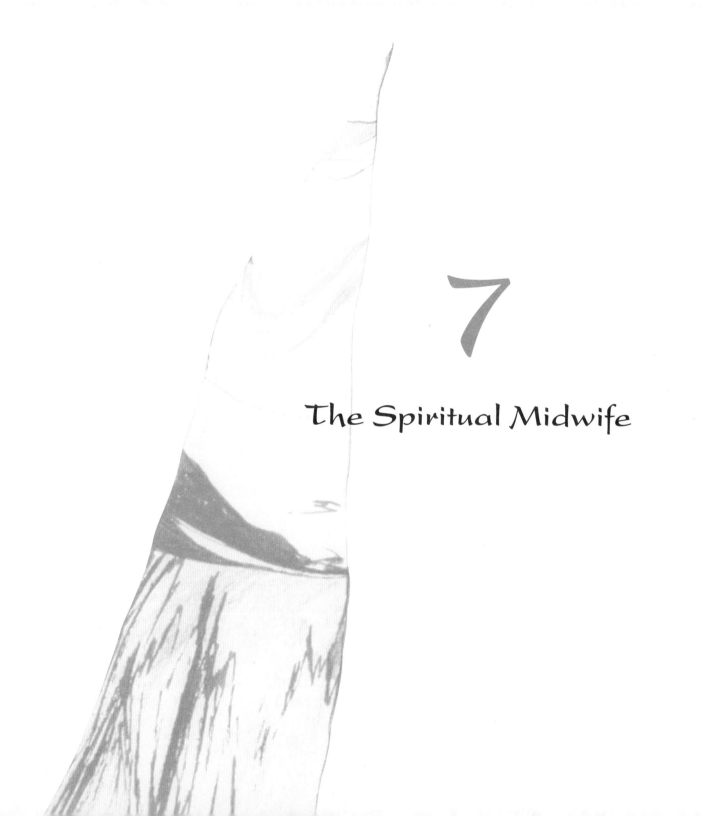

# 7

## The Spiritual Midwife

# Instructions to the Spiritual Midwife

*I ask that you take special care to prepare the site of the birthing. Burn a violet flame [ignite a tsp. of alcohol in a mound of Epsom salt], sage, or rosemary, if you prefer, to release and dissipate any old, stale energies. Then burn lavender or violet essence to set the pattern for the Violet Ray, which will transmute any energies released in the process. Sprinkle the floor with salt to absorb any misqualified energies which may be released. The room should be softly lit. Baths and showers may assist the Mother in relaxation and soothing emotional tensions. If the mother is uncomfortably hot, and baths are unavailable, sponge her with salt water and iodine, followed by clear water. Play soft music if she agrees. Remember the mother is to be the guide; allow her to determine any choices. Allow her to find the most opportune and appropriate position for herself. Accommodate her. Each birth is individual: remember this always.*

*At the beginning of labor, ask the mother and all present to ground to the planet and connect to the Source. Call forth assistance and protection from your personal guides, the Hierarchy, St. Germaine, and myself. Contact the soul of the child, speak to him/her of your desire to participate in a gentle, sacred birthing process. Ask the child of his/her needs and desires and ask for the name; get a consensus between the parents and yourself about this child. Remember, Dear One, you are to hold the focus of Light for this soul as it crosses through the transition. Prepare yourself and focus with the perfect intention of Love. Together, speak thusly to the child:*

*(all present) together, speak ....*

## During Labor: Before the Birth

*We (I) guide you forward into this form*
*we have created for you, out of Love.*
*You are a unique and special Being.*
*We ask that you come forward*
*at the precise moment of your choosing —*
*unified — a complete whole, Holy Being —*
*One of the Father, One of the Mother,*
*Ever connected now  and for eternity.*
*Blessed Holy Being ..............(name).*
*Come forward now and walk upon this Earth with me.*
*I bring you forth on the Wings of the Dove.*
*Born of this New Age, spirited and enlightened.*
*A Violet Babe, freedom alight and alive,*
*brought forth into form,*
*to live as love in action*
*Violet Light in Divine Form.*

Lady Master Portia

# During the Birth

*I wish to speak to you further of this Seventh Manu, [and the process of] assisting these Babes of Light on their journey into physical form. As they move through this transition point spoken of by beloved Sananda and Mary, they will be at once their most powerful self and their most vulnerable. It is important that the spiritual midwife, the focus point, be clear and present, that s/he constantly be speaking and assuring this Being. S/he may use the words "Om Manoya Potoya Hitaka,"[1] to remind the Being of his/her Infinite Presence. Draw a protective sphere surrounded by a figure eight, in gold and ruby red, representing the connection to the Celestial Realms and the Earthly Realm. Speak these words at the time of birth itself:*

---

[1]  Sanskrit phrase meaning, "I Am eternally protected"
[2]  Sanskrit phrase meaning, "I Am living life for the Lord of Light, Lord Maitreya."

# During the Birth

*I AM an Infinite Being, a Child of the Universe,*
*perpetually connected to the One, of the One —*
*manifesting in  infinite perfection in this earthly body.*
*Here upon this plane I will be known as ......(name). I AM a child of God,*
*Manifest in HUman form.*
*I AM a Co-creator,*
*incarnate on this plane to spread the Blessings*
*of the Universe — the Eternal Source —*
*the Beginning and the End — the Alpha and Omega —*
*the Light and the Dark,*
*To all that I see, touch, feel, heal and experience.*
*I AM eternally perfect in this form*
*that you, my parents have so lovingly created for me.*
*This form is of our choosing,*
*it is perfect and complete as I AM.*
*Love me as you do this very moment.*
*Feel my Love, a gift to you from the Universe*
*as you provide this most perfect gift for me.*
*We are the perfection of Love in form. Love in Action.*
*We are the harbingers of the*
*New Age of Spiritual Freedom.*
*Om Aloeha An Maitreya[2].*
*I AM the Living Breathing Love of GOD.*
*I AM ..........(name)*

Lady Master Portia

# 8

## Of Water Births
## and the Dolphins

# Of Water Births and the Dolphins

*Dear One, I AM your brother El Morya,[1] and I come forth as you have requested with information about our dear brothers and sisters, the dolphins, and how their presence here on this planet impacts [upon] the material you now bring forth concerning the Seventh Manu. These beings, the Blues, [he's showing me whales, dolphins, and manatees] came forward at the very beginning of creation on this planet, as they represent the virtues and attributes of the First Ray. They come forth from our sister planet Antarion (meaning opposite Orion), the third planet of the star system Sirius.[2] Each major star system has planets which parallel those in other systems; this one also parallels Antares in the Pleiades system. This planet, being closer to the Great Central Sun, has progressed through the same stages as Earth is now [moving through], and is very concerned with her well-being (for as you understand, each and every moment in the Universe affects all others). Understand that some aspects, being directly aligned, are even more affected or more influenced. Of course, this is by choice and agreement, always. The collective of beings on Antarion have agreed to send and maintain the Blues on Earth. The whales support the qualities of the Will of God, as represented through the recording and memory of the Truth. The joyful expression of the Will of God is represented by the dolphins, and the acceptance of the Will of God is maintained by the manatees.*

*Since it is the Will of God that babies on this planet come into beingness here (through the birth process) in a loving, gentle, joyous way, the dolphins have agreed to facilitate this process. They have given information to specific people to assist in the birthing process, to allow these Beings of Light of the Seventh Manu (who come to complete the cycle for this octave of the third dimension) to maintain their connection to the Universal Life Force, Prana, and to maintain a breathing pattern which will keep them intrinsically connected to the Source of All.[3]*

*If it is possible, the birthing process should be in the sea, in warm, clean ocean water, and the dolphins will come themselves and facilitate the birthing process. They will gently massage the mother and radiate high frequencies of energy to infuse the parents and the baby as it is being born. If this is prohibitive, the next best situation would be a birthing in saline solution with iodine for sterility and balance. Play dolphin and whale sounds and tapes underwater, and have the father or midwife massage these points.*

---

[1]   Master El Morya is the Chohan of the First Ray, the Blue Ray of Truth, Justice, and the Will of God.

[2]   The Mayans have long held that our star system spirals with Sirius in a double helical pattern around the center of the galaxy.

[3]   See also: Chris Griscom's book *Ocean Born*, 1989, Tim Wyllie's *Dolphins, Telepathy, and Underwater Birthing;* and Dr. Donald Epstein's *Network Chiropractic Technique* for clearing spinal and neural pathways (channeled by the dolphins).

*If an underwater birth is not possible, frequent bathing during labor will assist with relaxation and balance. These pressure points will greatly relieve stress and pain. I ask you, Dear One, to allow the Divine Will of God to come forth in the most natural and gentle way that is possible. If you assist and train these mothers and fathers in these meditations and techniques, you will be amazed at the transformation that will take place in the process of birth. In the last twenty years, the transition has been made from viewing birth as a manipulated, controlled, surgical procedure to seeing the natural process and celebration. If you consciously bring forth the radiance of the Spiritual Hierarchy into the birthing spaces, you will restablish birth as a sacred event, connecting man to the Universal consciousness of the All. Together we will bring forth a new generation to complete the cycle and move forward into the New Age of Peace and Harmony, where everyone will understand their connection to the Universal One.*

El Morya

# 9

## After the Birth............

# Eternally Connected

*I speak to you of Love and Devotion — Love, the vibration that binds us all, the very essence of life. This life source is an energy so simple and basic and yet so complex and subtle, it eludes many.*

*You have often experienced a bird or a child who can sing or play seemingly endlessly, pouring love forth freely to give to all. And yet the slightest negative thought, sharp word, or scowling look can silence this little one, making it close off or cry from pain. Little ones are especially sensitive to all energies. If treated with respect and honor, they will continue this sensitivity and honor all they encounter. If treated **without** conscious intention [which is] always infused with love, they will withdraw and become disconnected from their path and purpose.*

*I ask that you all consider two things,[two] practices, that if done will speed the evolution of this planet and make each being feel as an individual contributor:*

*   **Balance the energies in your children daily** *(this can also be done with anyone). Say unto them the following invocation [she's showing me how she stood or sat with Jesus facing her, holding his hands and looking into his eyes. One can have the child sit on the lap or stand touching toes to toes].*

*As you do this, run energy up through your feet, and down through the top of your head into your heart, out your hands and into the child's hands, into the heart and down into the feet, and then circle again. In this way, the child will feel energy flow through his/her body and cycle through another being and flow back into their own being. As s/he gets older have her/him reverse the cycle back to you. As you say these words, project energy from your heart and envision pink-gold light flowing into and encircling the child.*

Mother Mary

## Eternally Connected

*I AM the Light of God that Never Fails.*
*The Power of the Universe.*
*Dancing upon this Earth,*
*I AM a Being of Joy and Love for all to see.*
*Because I AM perfect in every way, every thought,*
*feeling and deed,*

# Plant a garden inside your heart

*The garden meditation is a wondrous practice. Here is how I was taught by the Elohim in the temples: Sit quietly and become still. Breathe deeply. Go into the garden. Imagine it a lovely spring day, soft and clear, sunny and bright, the temperature warm and yet the breeze like soft baby kisses on your arms. Remember this magical garden is yours alone. You can build it and plant it, just as you like it. It can be simple or complex, ordered and neat or wild as a meadow, jungle, or forest. First imagine it as a barren piece of earth. Divide some part of it into four sections. Plant a favorite plant or seed in the center of each one. Pat dirt upon it and then sit down upon it. Send the energy from the crown chakra down through your body into the seed to grow [if it is a plant, sit in front of it and project energy from your heart or your hands], then feel the energy of the earth and seed come back to you and cycle it again. Now plant this garden at your own pace. It is a magical garden. It can grow as slow or as fast as you desire. Plants can spring up at your fingertips or take months to mature. Each day when you come to visit, in some way pour your energy into the plants, tend them, weed [around] them, plant more, trim, or rearrange. Or just lovingly caress them, pat them, sing to them, or sit quietly projecting your love intently upon them. Watch them grow, flower, and mature.  And then sit in a receiving mode. Ever so quietly, sit or stand and open your energy centers in your feet and hands and heart, and feel the plants give back to you. Close your eyes and feel the energy enter your body and watch the pictures that happen inside your head or heart and hear the words or songs they sing. This garden is what you create. It can be pristine and simple like a Zen garden, have paths and ponds, waterfalls, trees, statues, structures or buildings. Whatever you wish.  It can change shape daily or even moment to moment. Just remember to create an exchange. We have so often forgotten why the plants are present on this planet for us. They cycle our energy, complete the cycle here on this Earth. They take our breath and convert it back to oxygen. They take our wastes and convert them back to minerals. They take the sun's energy and make food, energy for us to eat. They can do this in the most basic sense with energy. They can transmute and requalify energy immediately; it is how they are designed. Work in cooperation with them, as they are designed, and assist them in fufilling their purpose, as they assist you.*

*By creating this exchange you are re-creating the co-creative dance of the Angelic Realm and the Elemental Kingdom, male and female, yin and yang. Reset the focus for this, teach it to your children, and the world will fall into balance once more. Thank you for spending this time with me. I will come to you in your garden. Pray for the seasons, now and at the hour of all birth.*

I AM your loving sister and Mother of All, Mary

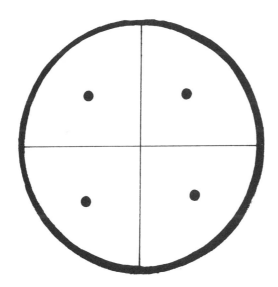

# On Approval:

**The act of verifying, bestowing assurance, and fostering self-esteem**

*Approval is what all of you Americans seek and value most. This is actually a very natural thing, for to find approval is to find verification of one's existence on the physical plane. Children seek approval all the time: they look to their mother's and their father's eyes to verify their experience. As a Light Being, living in a physical body for many of you is a very odd, dissonant experience. One must slowly and carefully learn the rules — the natural laws of the third dimension. As a baby does this, feeling and sensing his/her way, compiling experiences, s/he looks to a parent to verify that what is observed, actually is. If one gets feedback the experience will continue to unfold a trust, both between the parents and the child and also between the child and the experience, the child and his/her relationship with the planet. Some children in your country are left alone for hours and hours at a time. They have a large stockpile of experiences to validate. When they are with the parents, each interaction can create an opportunity to verify their experience. If they find approval, they will generalize this to other experiences. If they find disapproval and ridicule, [or] judgment, this will be generalized also. Soon they will question their very experience here. I am sure you know many Americans who question their existence, their purpose here, who do not trust this world, who seek approval from their peers. There are others who confidently move through the world never doubting experience, building one upon another, trusting their instincts. This is because at a very early age, possibly from birth, their experiences found approval. They verified their sensory input as it developed. Yes, it is true that each human chooses his/her birth family. And in doing so chooses, in essence, parents who presently have or will develope the ability and understanding to show approval. Many of you did not get this approval yourself, and I come forth and ask you to consider giving this gift to your children. It will speed their evolution and the evolution of the planet. This approval is a high form of love. It is a fine energy, one of attunement and attention.*

*It seems you Americans have often studied books to gain this approval. Yes, this is possible for one who can read and remember it. It is only one perspective you gain, one based on another's implied experience. As you find and re-establish your connection to the Source, you often seek approval there, from your guides and the angels. You will always find it. Some children find it from the Hierarchy directly. Oftentimes, this is their only source for many years. And then when they begin to speak, they mention — they talk about their guides, unseen by the parents — and are told not to believe. They are told that the source of their love, their approval, is not valid or does not exist. This may have happened to many of you. Imagine the dissonance. Here you have established a relationship, based on pure love (for that is all we ever give), constant attention, and approval. The third-dimensional guides, parents, or sponsors deny or disapprove — hold back their love if you speak of this relationship or continue it overtly. Many of you have continued these relationships; others cut them off in fear, fear [of] the loss of approval from the third-dimensional sponsors. This is the basis of much of the dysfunction you see. This is often what is supplied by what you call therapists who act and react with approval, filling in the gaps unfilled by parents. If they also allow and encourage a connection to the Source, they will help create balance and harmony within those they counsel.*

*Babies only cry when something in their immediate world (physically or energetically) is out of alignment. Physical needs — hunger, thirst, sleep, or comfort — if not satisfied will elicit a cry from an infant. What few people realize is that babies also respond to energy and therefore emotions and thoughts. If the parents or siblings are scared or angry, the baby will feel this. If there is tension or very high energy of a positive or negative nature in a room or house, a baby will respond.*

*When a baby is born, s/he does not have completely developed energy fields or auras, as we call them.[1] In order to be present in the third dimension, one must have the first three layers of the field present and fully functioning. Many of these Seventh Manu children will have four layers present at birth; most children have only three. Regardless, all children rely on their parents or whomever is caring for them or holding them to supply and fulfill the remainder of the energy fields. This is why separation is so traumatic for an infant. It is also why in most cultures around the world, babies are with their mothers all of the time [the image of a Native American papoose or an African baby in a hip sling came to my mind]. At between three and five months, the fourth layer will come forth and the baby will now have a completed design plan (often referred to as a belief system), the belief that they can exist without another's fields surrounding them. [Most parents have discovered that infants will sleep peacefully alone, and cry immediately upon awakening. At some magic moment around four months of age, they will walk into the nursery and the baby has awakened and is not crying! This is because the fourth layer is now functioning and the baby* **believes** *that Mom or Dad will return.]*

---

[1]   All beings incarnate on the earth have at least 7 layers to the auric field. Some have many more depending on experience in past lives. Most beings fields are fully functioning at age 7 — some take more time and all can develop and maintain higher levels thru spiritual discipline and evolution.

*Yes, your children [my personal children] are an interesting example. As very young babes, they found this attunement and approval from you. You kept them near to you almost always, [and] attended to them immediately when they cried. They learned to trust that the world was a comforting, safe place. Especially your son [my firstborn], for he was alone at first. You gave them tremendous energy, all of them, as much as you were able. You are understanding this now, energetically, yes. As they grew older, their father's way was different. Yes, it often included judgment — both the approval and the judgment had great intensity when given — but [they] were seemingly random, at times creating inconsistencies within their actual experiences. This is because of what he experienced as a child. So your children sought clarity. As they were denied your presence at times after you and their father split apart, they sought total attention from you when [you] were present. Difficult, as there were four now and all competing for your energy and approval. This is why you felt so pulled apart. This is why when you could spend time alone, one on one, with them, especially the younger two, it worked better. When they would come back to you, you would reestablish or validate their connection to the world. Yes, what they were experiencing was indeed happening, even if it was unpleasant. This is why they insisted upon telling you every detail of the time spent apart from you. Pain always develops from such questioning, left unanswered. One either separates from the other dimensions or disconnects from the worldly experience, if one can not have his/her experience validated.*

Now I asked about what will happen when these children of the Seventh Manu go out into world, where they will find disapproval and inconsistency.

*This will be difficult, yet it can be successful if they are prepared and **this experience also finds approval**, if it is explained that others are different (without judgment) that if the parent isn't present, they have only to seek guidance from their guides or angels. They must be prepared for the world. If they are accompanied and travel in the world with their parents, given explanations and guidance as they go, this would help.*

A dear friend of mine, Flo Calhoun, has channeled information from her guides, The Nameless Ones, about the critical time from birth to two years. In a wonderful tape[2] of a discussion with several mothers, she explains how to visualize places and experiences for the child, in preparation for going out in the world. Even for infants, this will allow them to prepare themselves energetically for noise, people, and change. If the experience plays out differently from what you planned, take a moment to validate the change in atmosphere for the child. In essence, maintain a verbal, visual, and telepathic communication with the child that verifies the energy of the experience. How often did you experience feeling things in a situation that went unexplained, especially unpleasant tense energies? If you are honest and stay centered and non-judgemental, able to observe and be forthright with the child, at least the experience is validated. Whatever happens is experienced as real, with honesty and without unanswered questions which allow judgments and fantasies to be filled in later.

*When they are old enough to play happily and quietly alone, encourage this. As they grow older, they must be taught how to reconnect to the Source, by themselves, to meditate, to find quiet time. This must be provided for them on a regular basis. The nap ritual, so common to American upbringing, is that. It is necessary even if the child does not sleep: the child must cultivate his/her own way of being without the parents present, yet close by. This is done at this time and the parent also has time to be alone, to reconnect to the Source.*

Mother Mary

---

[2] "Birth to Two Years," Flo Calhoun, New World Publishing, (203) 226-5060

## Sleep, Little One,

*Sleep, little one, sleep.*
*Grow,*
*accept this perfect body,*
*Baby of Light.*

> *Baby of mine,*
> *entrusted to me*
> *but for a moment,*
> *Living Divine Rite.*

> > *Child of All,*
> > *one with the spheres.*
> > *Precious, wondrous,*
> > *perfect, unique.*
> > *Whole and connected eternally.*

> *Explore this world with me:*
> *Eat the dirt,*
> *drink the rain,*
> *feel the fire,*
> *float on the wind,*
> *dance in the sun.*

> > *Child of the Garden,*
> > *Sing with the birds,*
> > *grass, cool, between your toes.*
> > *Play with the pups,*
> > *elephants and squirrels.*

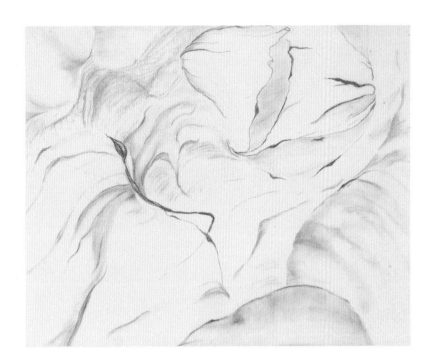

Babe of the Flowers,
inhale the perfume,
explore their petals,
stamen, and stalk —
the example of balance,
earthbound form.

Sleep little one, sleep,
for tomorrow is here!
You dance in the ONE
Circle of the Spheres,
Earthbound JOY
Heaven on Earth.

# Left Alone

Little one, you seem so sad
that life is as it seems —
the touch, the love withdrawn at times,
and still your light,
it beams. They roam and fly,
here and there, leaving you aloft.
They go in search of love, afar
and here you sit alone,
unknowing of who they are.

Close your eyes and think
of Me, the Great, Eternal One,
the essence of life in all to see, through eyes
who speak from hearts.

Oh little one, beauty bright,
glowing in all your splendor —
sit still, assured, and trust your sight;
for they return upon the morrow.
Question not their seeming flight,
for they so dearly love you.
Like breath and sound in waves they play,
in and out … "Oh, **stay,**" you say,
"see me here.

I hold the space for you to fly.
I hold the light for you to be
while moving off, adrift, at sea.

"Come home and hold me,
in your arms, so soft and tight.
Cradle me, gentle and bright —
and rock me free. Shine your light,
so I might see a reflection of you in me. For I
AM the child inside your heart, the flame
of love, embraced by all. The One,
the many, alone — alight.
I AM your heart, connected to all,
God's Holy Might."

10

# A New Way of Being

# A New Way of Being

*And so, my Dear Ones, you have experienced the possibility of a different kind of birth: a sacred event where time and intention are purposeful and respectful of each and every whisper and interaction. Each birth will unfold in its own particular manner; no two are the same. This honor and sacredness will set in motion a trust. Babes born in this way begin life on this Earth in harmony, listened to and trusting that they are integrated and supported. Continue as you have begun. Listen to the book of knowledge in your heart. As others give you information, listen respectfully, for it is **their** truth. Then take the time and reflect it against what is in your heart. If it rings true, in harmony, consider it. If not, choose other, as this is your truth. Listen always to your little ones and weigh this truth also, for they will test your limits and boundaries. You, after all, have more experience in this world and must look to their safety.*

I once asked St. Germaine's advice on how to assist my son through a crisis and he replied: *Dear One, what has been your experience with me as your guide and teacher when you come to me distraught ?*

"Well, you usually tell me a story from your own experience and then remind me of a time when things worked out well, when I accomplished my directive. You never judge my actions either way and since I can never hide from you, you will always know what has happened. I never feel the need to defend or explain myself with you. Somehow, your story makes me feel strong and wise and powerful. I forget how confused and awful I was feeling and I am able to face whatever I need to do and just **do it.**"

*Yes, Dear One, through relating a personal experience without judgment but rather locating the strength, power, and perfection in the person and re-enlivening it, you are able to activate their actions in an integrated manner. You can reflect their being back, like a mirror; the person can see who they truly are. They then have the vision of an empowered self, to begin to move into action. The lesson or moral can be taught in a story, a myth, or metaphor, without blame*

*— hopefully with humor. This allows the emotional layer to release the shame or guilt. Approaching someone without judgment allows you to approach and enter their energy fields without eliciting a defensive reaction. If you then fill their fields with pure love, you will set up a higher vibration, assisting them in clarity. If you allow yourself to experience learning also, you will both be filled with gratitude, a higher vibration will have been established for both of you and the will **to do** will be strong.*

*Laughter, music, warm baths with lavender, sunshine, hugs, and tickling are my best advice — and a sense of perspective. The Divine Plan is always in place; it is just often very hard to see how a given event, a seeming trial or trauma can be a lesson. Show your children by example, the best teacher.*

St. Germaine

# 11

## Spiritual ReBirthing

# ReBirthing

Upon reading this book, many friends have asked me to assist in their personal spiritual rebirthing. The Masters have given me the following instructions for those interested in this step in their evolutionary process. It is especially helpful for people who have had traumatic births or have strong feelings of lack of identity or a feeling of being uncomfortable on the planet. These and many other aspects of the personality and behavior can be traced to difficult, unwanted, ambivalent pregnancies or births, where anesthetics or forcible means were employed.

*Rebirthing is a re-enactment, energetically, of the transition and birth into physical form, which facilitates a release of energetic blocks or tensions caused by physical traumas or misplaced decisions which resulted in confusion, abrupt changes, or the use of toxic substances to alleviate fear, projected pain, and resistance. We ask you to consider the presence of a facilitator, a spiritual midwife, who can "see,"[1] determine blockages, and guide their release. This will result in a dramatic change in the energetic structure. The entity must be in agreement, WILLFULLY agreeing to change patterns and behaviors created by these blocks. Clearing these blockages will allow energetic matrixes and patterns to realign with the original design plan for this embodiment. The entity must understand, therefore, that life patterns and relationships which do not serve this plan may now become dissonant and fall by the wayside.*

*The process will be greatly facilitated if the room or area to be used is cleared energetically by the use of the Violet Flame, physically by burning sage or another violet incense, or [by burning] alcohol which has been placed in salt. This is a sacred event and should be treated as such; the space must be private and conducive to spiritual and healing energy. The words "Om Maneya Potoya Hitaka" should be toned. The floor may be salted. All present should purify their energetic fields, before and immediately after by immersing themselves in a salt bath within which seven drops of atomic iodine have been placed.[2] The spiritual midwife shall visualize a Violet Light surrounding the entity who has chosen to be transformed, and incant these words:*

---

[1]   Someone who has prepared themselves by clearing their own birth traumas, who can hold safe space and has active "inner vision."
[2]   Atomic iodine is ionized iodine, prepared according to Edgar Cayce's direction obtained through channeling. Available through Heritage Store, Virginia Beach, VA.

**I AM the Presence Commanding the Violet Flame to come forth and transmute and requalify any and all negative patterns and behaviors, their memory, causes, and effects resulting from this Being's birth process into physical form.**

*Use slow, deep, controlled breathing to accompany a meditation designed to guide this person backward through time to his/her birth. Allow him/her to experience the full range of sensations and emotions, assisting the release of unwanted patterns. Energy matrixes should be realigned and visualized as perfect and whole. Several sessions may be necessary to establish a space of trust and safety, each session delving more deeply backwards in time. If possible, move to the period in utero and of conception, as often energies projected at these times are important. A practitioner trained in spiritual rebirthing, energy release work, Ascended Masters' Free Energy Techniques, Reiki, or similar dispensation may assist this process.*

Lady Master Portia

# Reborn

*To feel the love of All*
*coursing through*
*my being, connected again,*
*as never before. I'm soft pink*
*unfolded, enfolded within*
*her arms — my mother*
*Mary, mother of All.*
*She sings a lullaby*
*and cradles my head*
*and I stretch and reach.*
*Look to the Light*
*Father bright, protecting*
*Love of All, you enshroud*
*me in Light. To grow*
*brighter, wiser, seeing*
*All there is. Woven*
*together. Threads of silver*
*Gold and Blue. The Will*
*of God, coursing*
*through All, Who ...*
*HU the sound emerges.*
*A whisper, a Roar*
*One Heartbeat together*
*Eternally One.*

# 12

## Living in the Breath, Sound, and Light

## Living in the Breath, Sound, and Light

Everything in the Universe is comprised of energy. The New Physics — quantum and systems theories — has now confirmed what metaphysicians, theosophists, and alchemists have long taught: that this energy and the space it moves in is what makes up the Universe and all its parts. We are inexplicably interconnected, and yet the individual is critical to the formation of systems which determine the form energy will take. Energy can particularize as atoms and molecules, bone, feathers, bark, and whales, or be present as waves, photons, gammas, and ultraviolets. The Spiritual Hierarchy teaches that "the World was created in Seven Rays of Breath, Sound, and Light." Our third-dimensional experience corresponds to these three aspects of energy, which correlate with the Triune, reflected in our concepts of God, across all cultures and religions, from the mysteries of the Ancients to the modern New Age.

| Breath | Sound | Light |
|---|---|---|
| child aspect | female aspect | male aspect |
| action | feeling | thought |
| power | unconditional love | wisdom |
| blue | pink | yellow-gold |
| 1st auric layer | 2nd auric layer | 3rd auric layer |

Without any and all of these three aspects, one cannot imagine life in the third dimension. It is when we begin to balance and **consciously** manipulate these three dimensions, according to Universal Law and Natural Order, that we begin to understand becoming the God-Beings we truly are. We have all experienced other dimensions, unseen as yet by most waking eyes, and yet so profound that we all crave them. As we sleep and meditate, we glimpse many of these realms, and bring back visions and messages to enhance and guide us on our journey.

All beings incarnate on the Earth at this time have at least seven layers to their energy fields; many beings have more. Great master/teachers can have as many as seventeen. These fields surround the physical body, interact with it constantly, exchanging energy and information. Each layer has tiny filaments and matrixes (unseen by the human eye) which connect and transfer energy through and between all the systems. The three layers closest to the physical body correspond to the breath, sound, and light. They are the slowest in vibration and actually allow us to function on this plane. The fourth layer contains the blueprints for this incarnation and is encoded with our embodiement plan and purpose. The fifth, sixth, and seventh layers connect us to the Spiritual Realms and contain reconds of our past lives, experiences from other realms, soul systems, and potential.

The Ascended Masters teach us that we must master the third -dimensional experience before we can begin to realize waking movement into these other realms. The Babes of the Seventh Manu are being sent to guide us through the final stages of the transition through the known world of the third density and into the heightened experiences of the unknown realms of higher dimensions. As we begin to prepare ourselves for the birthing and raising of the Babes of the Seventh Manu, we must begin to look at this world through their perspective and see the perfection and balance that they experience. Life is simple and balanced for them. They experience the sweetness of each breath of Life Force, the melody and harmonies of the Symphony of the Spheres, and the full spectrum of the Light of God that Never Fails.[1] By bringing perfected aspects of these frequencies into our homes and lives, we will reflect that which these babes know to be true. We will also heighten our own life in this third-dimensional experience.

---

[1]  Life Force — Prana: Universal energy, love energy. Symphony of the Spheres - the patterns and geometry of the Universe, the sun and planets, often said to be recollected in music.
The Light of God that Never Fails - the ever expanding all presence of God, the Source, the One.

*Dear Ones, I AM Sanat Kumara, and I wish to speak to you of Love and how it is interconnected with the concept of the Triune: the Love of the Father, the Love of the Mother, and the Love of the Child. Many of those on your planet today have ambivalence about this Love. They are not certain if any or all of these aspects of Divinity truly exist. The Love, Wisdom, and Power of the third aspect, the Child, is rarely acknowledged. The Holy Ghost or Spirit as embodied by Christ, the Dolphin, or Jesus, in many ways is easier for many to grasp. In actuality, it represents the Child aspect of Divinity. The emotional body has a soft feeling for the Child, and yet the concepts of Mother and Father are so closely tied to the memory of the primary family in this and other lifetimes, that ambivalence or anger is the response often elicited by mention of the words. It is acknowledgment of all three aspects, balanced within each individual being, that allows access to the qualities of Divine Wisdom, Divine Power, and Divine Love. One must accept and love all three aspects within, and the reflection in the genders of our brothers, sisters and children, without. Only when we approach these aspects in everyone can we accept the Divine in Self.*

*Assist your brothers and sisters by tuning into these aspects through prayer and meditation. Address them regularly and they will speak to you. By enrolling the three aspects of the Universal Consciousness, the One, which correspond to that of the third dimension, you will be guided as to how you can express yourself in service to the Universal through the power of the Breath, Sound, and Light, to employ Infinite Love and Infinite Wisdom.*

Sanat Kumara

# Breath

Breathing is an unconscious act for most of us. We know that without breath there is no life, and yet we as a species have long forgotten how to breathe the life energy that is available to us with every breath of air. All wild animals breathe oxygen and also breathe Prana. Prana is the Hindu word for life force (<u>Chi</u>, in China; <u>Ki</u>, in Japan; "orgone" as termed by Tesla and others)-the unseen energy ambient in all environments. Nicholas Tesla documented the evidence of this pulsing energy and called it orgone. He was able to create a machine to increase or decrease the ambient orgone and affect its organization. We humans are also designed to utilize this orgone or Prana energy, through our subtle energy bodies and the chakra system. By learning to consciously breathe, we utilize our entire lung capacity, making our physical engines and systems run efficiently. We avail ourselves of Prana and can find new vitality, health, and connection to life and the Source.

In ancient days we breathed Prana through our crown chakra and base chakra, utilizing the energy of the Sun (the Father) and the Earth (the Mother), enlivening the entire chakra system and therefore all the subtle energy systems. The solar energy came through the top of the head and passed through the pineal gland, the hypothalamus, and then into the throat, lungs, and heart. Most humans now breathe through their nose and mouths only, bypassing the two important systems governed by the pineal and the hypothalamus: the immune system and the subtle organs of perception, higher intuition, and inner vision.

The breath activates and clears the physical body; it corresponds to the first layer of the auric field. It is very powerful, if employed correctly for healing and maintaining health. Its power is immense and must be accompanied by pure thoughts and intention, for if misused it will lead to disastrous results. Breathwork can release energy patterns and blocks held in the physical body into the emotional field, creating pain and the sensation of strong feeling. One must learn how to completely ground and move these released patterns gently through the emotional field. Someone trained in transformational breathwork or rebirthing or yogic breathing should be present for you. First experiment with breathing and slowly learn how to move energy; you will be pleasantly surprised by the results. Always ask for guidance and protection, and use invocations, evoking the name of God, ask for the presence of your guiding and overlighting angels, elementals, and Masters, when doing any exercises or disciplines. You are using Universal Laws and subtle, powerful energies far greater than the third-dimensional mind can imagine. Protect yourself. Follow your guidance and intuition and breathe the Breath of Life.[2]

---

[2]  Imagine a golden cord running between the chrown chakra and the base chakra, a golden pulsing cord of Universal Life Force Energy.

# The Breath of Life

*Dear Ones, concentrate on this breathing, the Breath of Life. It is possible for you to retrain your physical body, as your subtle bodies and energy passages will remember very quickly. If you as parents learn to breathe Prana again, the labor and delivery will be greatly eased. Labor is just that: an act of willfully bringing forth a new life. As such, it requires vast amounts of energy. If you learn through breathing and meditation, alone and together, to access the free energy of the Earth, the Mother, herself, you will be infused with an unending source of pure life force to assist in this task.*

*Once your babe is born, probably the second greatest gift you can give him/her [the first is to surround the infant always in unconditional love], is the extension of Prana breathing. I will explain. All human babies breathe Prana naturally for between four and six weeks after birth. They gradually pattern their breath process after the mother, primarily, and forget to breathe through the golden cord. If the parents bring life force with every breath into their own golden cord, this is what the child will pattern to. This process can be facilitated by gently cradling your newborn with a hand on the head and a hand on the buttocks, engulfing the sacrum. Inhale and visualize golden light coming into your own body through the top of your head and your base chakra. Inhale slowly and deeply and feel the Life Energy engulfing your body, the two energies — from above and below — meeting in your heart. Now exhale and move the energy through your arms and hands and into your little one's body. After you are comfortable with the procedure, you can practice inhaling through the crown [chakra] and exhaling out through the base [chakra], for seven breaths, then reversing this for seven more breaths. As you do this, visualize the energy synchronized in your baby, moving with your breath through your hands. Do this daily, and begin to say the Prayer of the Cosmos at the same time to the little one. As s/he grows, sit him/her on your lap, breathing and praying together. Many little ones like it if you tone or sing the prayer. Imagine the bond you will create together, how you can utilize this connection for healing, peace, and communication. Soon you will experience a union of self with that of your child. You may do this as a couple with, both parents holding the child: father at the head and mother at the feet, duplicating the male-female polarity. Do this with other children and even adults to reactivate the flow of Prana through the golden cord. Each time you do, call upon the power of the Violet Ray; invoke the name of God, the Christ, St. Germaine and myself. This will assist in protecting your family and self and transmute any negative or misqualified energies into pure available Love.*

*Lady Master Portia*

# Sound

Sound is one of the vehicles most clearly tied to healing, particularly through the emotions. It activates and feeds the emotional body, the second layer of the human aura, releasing stored emotional blocks. How often have we burst into tears upon hearing a certain song? Sounds and music evoke strong images of past experiences. They are our most direct feeling experience of what vibration is. Everything in the Universe has a mapping of vibration, which includes a color, sound, and smell particular and unique to it. It is a harmonic blending, determined by molecular or wave structure and chemistry or composition. The subtle energy bodies, chakras, and meridians respond to sound; one can tune into the octave of each individual person. Each major chakra represents a step, beginning wtih the base chakra as the lowest. Babies are extremely sensitive to all vibration, particulary sound. Thomas Verney, in *The Secret Life of the Unborn Child*, tells a story of a cello player who instantly knew how to play particular pieces of music, before he could read, seemingly unknown before, only to find that his mother had played this music before he was born, but not afterward!

In *Healing Yourself During Pregnancy*, Joy Gardner-Gordon advises fathers to speak and sing to their children in uteri to increase the bond. Studies have shown that the unborn child actually hears its parents' voices, and when a father has spoken soothingly to his baby before birth, the newborn is able to pick out his/her father's voice across a room. This book also describes experiences utilizing toning to assist pregnancy, labor, and delivery. Garden-Gordon explains that a woman who is encouraged to express herself will make sounds during labor and delivery similar to having a prolonged orgasm. During delivery she may scream in pain or rapture. These sounds help to open and relax her pelvis and cervix.[3]

Perhaps the easiest thing for anyone to do is sing softly to a baby. This is far more balancing and healing than anyone can imagine. Toning can break up misaligned energy patterns and set in perfected ones. Most people who use tone in healing do it intuitively, so you probably are better at it than you think. Sets of tones or tunes can literally "tune up your aura." Sounds are the first thing that the human organism senses *in utero* and the last sense to leave a dying person. Sing, hum, and tone to your baby and s/he will sleep better and find the world a place of harmonious existence.

[3]   Joy Gardner-Gordon, *The Healing Voice*, chapter 12, *Toning for Birth* ,page 158.

# Light And Color

Light, the highest vibration of the third dimension corresponds to our mental layer, " I see the light," "the light dawns," "I knew in a flash" are all expressions which speak of our innate understanding of how our thoughts, are in fact, light. These thoughts move quickly, and because of the high rate of their vibrations, connect us to the higher realms.

Just as water seeks the highest level, so do we as humans (actually, complex bundles of energy) always seek higher energy levels. We call this process evolution. We experience it on a daily basis in our quest to be enlightened, feel the higher vibrations of joy and balance. Many of us have used drugs and chemicals to attempt to keep our vibrations "high." Higher vibrations influence lower vibrations, activating them and assisting them in establishing patterns which will allow higher levels of vibration to be established. Our thoughts or ideas are inititated in the third, mental layer. Once activated they move through and engage our emotions or the second layer, after which they become in the physical layer. The frequency of energy is progressively stepped down until it falls into the frequency of that which we know as matter. This can happen in a split second if our thoughts, feelings and actions are aligned, integrated and focused commmpletely. We call it manifestation. It is the power of our thoughts to create. The vision or dream of a choreographer becomes a dance. An architect draws up the plans for a building. An entrepreneur designs a new business. The information in this book takes this process into account. Ideas and thoughts are presented in channelings, expressed though the emotions in drawings, and enhanced by the word in poems, narratives and prayers. The Masters have requested that the prayers be spoken out loud, accompanied by visualizations in light and color, thus engaging the three layers: mental (light and color), emotional (sound and tone), and the physical (breath and speaking). When all are activated, we can create change on the physical plane,  change on the physical plane.

All of this is to explain the power of our thoughts. If we believe birth to be onerous and requiring suffering, it will be so. It may be that this is the experience that we need to grow and evolve. This is a choice, oftentimes made before the incarnation. Whatever one chooses is perfect and in Divine Order. Each of us needs different lessons, at different times. As Lord Sanada often says, "We all awaken; it is the timing that is the choice." The process presented in this book represents some of the possibilities, not the right ones or the only ones. If you hold a visualization of a healthy happy child, it will greatly facilitate your child's travel though the third-dimensional experience.

# Everyone Has a Song

The paper caught my eye from the floor as I walked down Joseph's hall. It had been an incredible afternoon,putting the poetry for Gabriel's Garden[4] on tape. I had started out with my stomach in my throat, and between Joseph's sweetness and encouragement and the magic that entered the room, the words had flowed in perfect time to the music, and now I was floating. The paper begged me to pick it up. It was a Buddhist journal filled with loving articles; the cover story an article on raising a child from a village perspective — an interesting article and yet, on the bottom of the page, was an old African folk tale that virtually sang to my heart.  My body tingled with excitement as I read on. I believe this tale was the genesis of this book and I share it with you from memory, for I have long since lost the journal and regrettably cannot attribute an author.

It seems that in a certain village in Africa, a young woman is guided to go into the forest, where she will hear a special song: the song of her unborn child. This song is easily remembered and, upon returning to the village, she sings it to the lucky man whom she chooses to become the father of her child. She teaches it to him and they sing it together as they conceive the child. The song is taught to the midwife and it is sung at the birth of their child. The entire village learns the song and as the child grows, it is repeated often. If s/he cries or becomes upset, falls or becomes hurt, whoever is nearby picks him/her up, cradles him/her and sings the song. It is sung at each ceremony, ritual, and rite of passage throughout the life, at the wedding, and for the final time at the person's death.

This story touched me deeply and I thought of how life would be in such a place, where an individual was honored and revered with a song, not just a name or number. So my friends, begin to listen for your song. I began to hear mine in the shower. It began as a progression of notes and some days it is a complete aria. Listen for the songs of those you love. Try a little experiment: if you hear one, try humming it. One time, my dear friend Rachel sang a tune to me during a healing session. She said it was for my heart, which was feeling a little injured from a recently terminated relationship. As she hummed the tune, I recognized it! I told her I sang it in the shower all the time. It was my song and it rapidly mended my heart!

---

[4]  *Gabriel's Garden* is a multimedia, interactive installation about the awakening process. It was co- created  by the author and the White Brotherhood in 1992.

# On Nutrition and Sleep

*Dear Ones, these little ones, the children of tomorrow, are now in your care and safekeeping. We in the other realms will watch over them closely, and assist in all that we can. If you choose to engage in the sacredness of life, maintaining your own connection to the Source and flooding them with love, patience, and harmony, they will blossom endlessly. We cannot disclose, as of now, their exact mission on the Earth. Suffice it to say that they will lead you all into a future of peace, love, and harmony, a virtual Heaven on Earth. My strongest advice as to how to assist them is to follow your intuition. Each child is an individual and as such will have strong and tenacious desires, needs, and tastes. All of the babes should be nurtured on [their] mother's milk, if at all possible, until they gradually wean themselves to other fluid and food. Meat should never be eaten. A simple diet of fresh fruits, vegetables, and whole grains is sufficient. Milk, butter, and eggs may agree with some of them. The personality ray of the embodiment[5] and starseed[6] will determine their tastes and nutritional requirements. Consult the Higher Self of the child at any time if their wants seem not to fit your intuition or beliefs. The life force is very strong in these Beings and will require food in which that force has been maintained. Food that has been grown with love and care, without the use of pesticides or chemicals, and allowed to ripen naturally and picked at the height of its season, is optimum. It is important that the genetic patterns have not been altered. Food absorbs the vibrations of those who handle and prepare it. If one cannot procure the best, freshest ingredients, infusing that which you have with love, care, and lifeforce can correct the imbalance. It is important, whenever possible, that food be prepared by hand with the purest intentions and love.*

*The subtle energy bodies of these babes will travel to many realms while they are sleeping and they will seem to be unable to be aroused. Do not be concerned; they will return when the physical body needs attending to. If you allow yourself to fall into their patterns of sleep and wakefulness, especially for the first four to five months, you, the primary caregiver, will fall into harmony also. It would be advisable to keep these babes within thirty-five feet of the mother or father whenever possible, particularly when wakeful. This will ensure that they will always feel whole and complete, for the parents' energy fields, in essence, support and fulfill the undeveloped fields of an infant.[7]*

Lady Master Portia

---

[5]  Each person embodies with an overriding frequency of vibration, corresponding to a color or harmony of colors. There is also a frequency which connects to the lifestream and the work which is to be focused on in this life time. See Appendex E Pg 124.

[6]  The starseed refers to the original 12 frequencies which came to the earth to blend with the mother frequency inherent here.

[7]  See page 87.

# Essences, Aroma Therapy, and Crystals

The use of various essences has been suggested during the birthing process and to assist in soothing and calming the infant after birth. "In this evolutionary plan, flowers were and are the very essence and the highest concentration of life force on the planet. They are the crowning experience of the plant's growth. They are a combination of etheric properties and are at the height of life force ... The actual essence, of course, is the electromagnetic pattern of the plant form. Even as there are nutritional elements found in various plant forms ye partake of for the physical body, so in turn are the various parameters of biomagnetic energies discharged by flowers and various plant forms."[8]

When flower essences are prepared with sunlight and water, they contain the perfection of a physical expression of life force on the planet. The vibration is transferred to the water, even without any of the plant material included, similar to homeopathic preparation. "Flower essences engage the subtle energies and vibration of the third through seventh layer of the field. They are of vital importance to whose who wish to introduce and utilize a pattern of perfection into their fields."[9]

*When trauma and stress create misalignments in the fields of these Babes of the Seventh Manu, they will find little solace or assistance in the traditional allelopathic medicine of the physical plane. Being of the Violet Ray, their energy bodies are fine and subtle, and will readily respond to light, color, vibrational, and electromagnetic healing therapies. Flower essences and aromas may be utilized to soothe, balance, and clear their fields, particularly if they are exposed to unconscious thoughts or dissonant noises, anger, depression, radiation or strong electromagnetic static. Bathe them in water or infuse the air with essences and aromas of lavender, violet, rose, or germander. The use of crystal and gem elixirs and applications of such preparations on the chakras and meridians may be utilized also. If they do fall in vibration or take on an illness or dis-ease, three drops of "VitaFons Water" on the tongue or "Bach" or "Peralandra"[10] essences applied as instructed may be utilized. Visualization and prayer is of great assistance, as well as hands-on healing and the channeling of energy and forms of electromagnetic realignment and balancing, in acute cases. If these babes become ill or injured, ask for assistance and guidance from the individual's Higher Self, their guides and sponsors, Lady Portia, and myself. Trust your own intuition and remember that they have made agreements to transmute various energies, patterns, and systems. Their presence and experience here is blessed, in alignment with the qualities of the Violet Ray and in Divine Perfect Order.*

St. Germaine

Aromatherapy can be very helpful also. It utilizes essential oils of a particular flower and, as such, includes the vibrational essence also. Essential oils my be easier to procure than pure essences. Be careful to use the highest quality you can find and always test the baby's sensitivity to the oil before infusing it.[11] Flower essences in water rarely elicit allergic or hypersensitive reactions.

Crystals and gems are of a very high vibrational frequency and also may be of assistance in realignment and healing. Gem elixirs are preparations where the vibrational pattern and the sacred geometric structures of specific crystals are transferred to water and infused with sunlight or moonlight. These are also used in healing and for balancing subtle energy fields and have been recommended for special cases in treatment with Seventh Manu children.

I have repeatedly experienced these children having a special attraction to flowers and crystals. A fellow Reiki Master and healer often brings his little boy to healing sessions or classes. When this child was a toddler — barely able to walk, not talking at all — he would meander around the room, selecting various items and bring them to me, pointing to places or placing them directly on his father. He never spoke a word but communicated through motion and telepathy. He would come over to me and take my hand and place it on a specific place on his own body that needed attention. If these children are allowed and encouraged to use their "other dimensional senses," they can teach us many wondrous lessons. Many of them talk freely about the angels and Masters that they see and communicate with, often telling their parents "messages" and relaying information from them. They often facilitate spontaneous healing in people who they meet. Many see auras and colors around people and will talk about it freely if encouraged. One little girl started playing with the meridians on her mom's feet after observing me clear them. She told me the colors and then was able to see the colors streaming from her own hands. Another child lay down on the floor below the healing table and began adjusting her sister's matrixes.[12] When asked why she was there, on the floor, she told us that it was "easier to see the lines on this side."

---

[8] Gurudas, Flower Essences and Vibrational Healing, channeled by Kevin Ryerson, Albuquerque, NM, Brotherhood of Life, Inc., 1981.

[9] St. Germaine, Healing with Subtle Energies, channeled by P. Greenwell, 1993.

[10] VitaFons, Bach, and Peralandra are all trade names for channeled preparations of flower essences; see Appendix.

[11] Use kinesiology or apply a drop on the forearm, if it becomes inflamed do not continue use.

[12] The auras or energy fields are held in place and energized by a system or matrix, much like how a filament carries the current in a light bulb. When a person is out of alignment, the matrixes are not ordered. Polarity, Seventh Ray Energetics, Reiki, Energy Balancing, and other systems directly or indirectly realign and balance these matrixes.

# Appendix A

*Greetings, my dear Ones. We speak in the forms most common to you. By this I mean we make ourselves known to you in the way that you will recognize us. As you know, we are actually Pillars of Light and have the ability to slow our vibrations at will because of our mastery achieved in the third dimension, even down to that of form. We bring this vibration slowly down to the threshold of the third dimension and, as you have raised your vibrations to that threshold, we can — in essence — communicate with you. Often times, the initial communications are through the Higher self through infusions and initiations of Light, or in dreams. After we have worked with you and realigned your fields so that your vibration can be safely raised to the threshold near to the speed of light, so that you will be able to "see" interdimensionally, we can language directly with you. Yes, this is done through the language of Light but dedicated channels will soon learn how to translate this into their personal language and idioms of the time. I come to this channel (Penny) and continue to come in the form most easily recognizable, that of Joseph and St. Germaine, for this lifestream spent time with me in these forms or bodies. The spelling of my name with an E is correct, as she has known me. It carries with it a more feminine vibration, necessary for her work. Be comfortable with its use, for it holds the vibration of my essence. In a later lifetime, the E was dropped because of common spelling at the time. It is in essence proper in both ways because of my acceptance.*

St. Germaine

# Appendix B

# Grounding Meditation

Take three deep cleansing breaths and center your attention on the area right below your sternum, the soft "V" formed by your ribs. Close your eyes and imagine three gold and ruby twisted cords, one coming from your base chakra and one from the bottom of each foot. With each exhalation, send these cords down through the floor and into the Earth: through the mud, rocks, and water, downward through the molten magma, all the way to the core of the planet, which is a bright golden light-filled spinning gyro. Keep going into the very center of the gyro, where you will find a tiny but very exquisite ruby. Send your cords right into the center of this ruby and attach them. Now bring the gold and ruby energy of the heart of the world back up through all the layers of the planet, up through the rocks and water and dirt and into your feet, up your legs, your thighs, into your hips, and torso and all the way into your heart. You feet will feel heavy, barely able to move. You may feel warm and filled with a deep sense of love. Now, with the next breath, feel golden, silver-white light entering the top of your head through your crown chakra. With each inhalation, bring this energy into your heart also. Feel it pass between your eyes, down the back of your sinuses, the back of your throat through your neck, into your chest and into your heart. Feel the two energies mix in your heart and feel your heart expand to encompass your whole being. Send energy out of your heart to others and the planet. If you wish to give healing energy to another person, rub your hands together and as you exhale, feel this blessed energy move down your arms, into your hands, and out the large chakra in the middle of each hand and down through to the tips of each finger.

Do this exercise when you meditate or pray, sending energy from your heart to others. If you feel any pain after you connect to the planet, exhale deliberately and channel the celestial energy (gold, silver-white light) through your crown chakra, all the way through your body, out of your base chakra, into the ground. Oftentimes this brings up feelings of fear and anxiety. Keep exhaling the glorious gold, silver-white energy and whisper " I AM eternally protected."